jQuery Essentials

Optimize and implement the features of jQuery to build
and maintain your websites with minimum hassle

Troy Miles

PUBLISHING

BIRMINGHAM - MUMBAI

jQuery Essentials

First published: January 2016

Production reference: 1220116

Published by Packt Publishing Ltd.
Livery Place
35 Livery Street
Birmingham B3 2PB, UK.

ISBN 978-1-78528-635-3

www.packtpub.com

Credits

Author
Troy Miles

Reviewers
Joydip Kanjilal
Anirudh Prabhu

Commissioning Editor
Edward Gordon

Acquisition Editor
Meeta Rajani

Content Development Editor
Kirti Patil

Technical Editor
Mohit Hassija

Copy Editor
Stuti Srivastava

Project Coordinator
Nidhi Joshi

Proofreader
Safis Editing

Indexer
Hemangini Bari

Graphics
Kirk D'Penha

Production Coordinator
Shantanu N. Zagade

Cover Work
Shantanu N. Zagade

About the Author

Troy Miles, a.k.a. the Rockncoder, began writing games in assembly language for early computers, such as the Apple II, Vic20, C64, and the IBM PC, over 35 years ago. Currently, he spends his days writing web apps for a Southern California-based automotive valuation and information company. During the nights and weekends, he can usually be found writing cool apps for mobile and Web or teaching other developers how to do that. He likes to post interesting code nuggets on his blog at http://therockncoder.com and videos on his YouTube channel at https://www.youtube.com/user/rockncoder. He can be reached at rockncoder@gmail.com.

About the Reviewers

Joydip Kanjilal is a Microsoft Most Valuable Professional in ASP.NET, speaker, and author of several books and articles. He has over 18 years of industry experience in IT with more than 10 years in Microsoft .NET and its related technologies. He was selected as MSDN Featured Developer of the Fortnight (MSDN) a number of times and also as Community Credit Winner at www.community-credit.com several times. He has authored the following books:

- *Entity Framework Tutorial Second Edition, Packt Publishing*
- *ASP.NET Web API – Build RESTful Web Applications and Services on the .NET Framework, Packt Publishing*
- *Visual Studio Six in One, Wrox Publishers*
- *ASP.NET 4.0 Programming, Mc-Graw Hill Publishing*
- *Entity Framework Tutorial, Packt Publishing*
- *Pro Sync Framework, APRESS*
- *Sams Teach Yourself ASP.NET Ajax in 24 Hours, Sams Publishing*
- *ASP.NET Data Presentation Controls Essentials, Packt Publishing*

Joydip has authored more than 300 articles for some of the most reputable sites, such as www.msdn.microsoft.com, www.code-magazine.com, www.asptoday.com, www.devx.com, www.ddj.com, www.aspalliance.com, www.aspnetpro.com, www.sql-server-performance.com, www.sswug.com, among others. A lot of these articles have been selected for www.asp.net: Microsoft's Official Site on ASP.NET.

He has years of experience in designing and architecting solutions for various domains. His technical strengths include C, C++, VC++, Java, C#, Microsoft .NET, Ajax, WCF, Web API, REST, SOA, Design Patterns, SQL Server, Operating Systems, and Computer Architecture.

He blogs at `http://aspadvice.com/blogs/joydip` and `http://www.infoworld.com/blog/microsoft-coder`. His website is located at `www.joydipkanjilal.com`. You can contact him on Twitter at `https://twitter.com/joydipkanjilal`, on Facebook at `https://www.facebook.com/joydipkanjilal`, and on LinkedIn at `http://in.linkedin.com/in/joydipkanjilal`.

Writing a book has always been a rewarding experience for me. My special thanks go to the entire Packt team for providing me with the opportunity to review this book. I am also thankful to the entire management team at SenecaGlobal for their continued support. My special thanks to my family for the continued inspiration and support. Thank you so much, all!

Anirudh Prabhu is a software engineer with over 5 years of industry experience.

He specializes in technologies such as HTML5, CSS3, PHP, jQuery, Twitter Bootstrap, and SASS, and he also has knowledge of CoffeeScript and AngularJS.

In addition to web development, he has been involved in building training material and writing tutorials for twenty19 (`http://www.twenty19.com/`) for the technologies that have been mentioned.

Anirudh has authored *Beginning CSS Preprocessors With Sass, Compass, and Less, Apress* (`http://www.apress.com/9781484213483`).

Besides Packt Publishing, he has been associated with Apress and Manning Publications as a technical reviewer for several titles.

www.PacktPub.com

Support files, eBooks, discount offers, and more

For support files and downloads related to your book, please visit www.PacktPub.com.

Did you know that Packt offers eBook versions of every book published, with PDF and ePub files available? You can upgrade to the eBook version at www.PacktPub.com and as a print book customer, you are entitled to a discount on the eBook copy. Get in touch with us at service@packtpub.com for more details.

At www.PacktPub.com, you can also read a collection of free technical articles, sign up for a range of free newsletters and receive exclusive discounts and offers on Packt books and eBooks.

https://www2.packtpub.com/books/subscription/packtlib

Do you need instant solutions to your IT questions? PacktLib is Packt's online digital book library. Here, you can search, access, and read Packt's entire library of books.

Why subscribe?

- Fully searchable across every book published by Packt
- Copy and paste, print, and bookmark content
- On demand and accessible via a web browser

Free access for Packt account holders

If you have an account with Packt at www.PacktPub.com, you can use this to access PacktLib today and view 9 entirely free books. Simply use your login credentials for immediate access.

Table of Contents

Preface

jQuery Essentials helps you master the core capabilities of the most popular open source libraries ever created. You'll start by understanding the most fundamental parts of jQuery: selectors and filters. From selectors, you learn DOM manipulation, events, form validation, and more. To keep your site running fast, you'll have to measure its performance and improve it. Along the way, we'll show you lots of easy-to-remember best practices. In the end, you'll be able to make your site snazzier than ever with jQuery.

What this book covers

Chapter 1, jQuery Part by Part, provides a quick introduction to jQuery along with information on why it was created.

Chapter 2, jQuery Selectors and Filters, shows how to use jQuery's most fundamental capability: querying the Document Object Model, or DOM.

Chapter 3, Manipulating the DOM, walks you through the various ways in which jQuery can be used to modify and replace elements on screen.

Chapter 4, Events, explains how to make your site dynamic by using events to respond to interactions by users and systems.

Chapter 5, Making Your Site Snazzy with jQuery, takes a look at ways to use animation to make your site lively.

Chapter 6, Better Forms with jQuery, provides examples and explanations on using jQuery to process and validate user form data before sending it to a server.

Chapter 7, Talking to Your Server, dives into using Ajax to send and retrieve data from your server.

Chapter 8, Writing Code that You can Read Later, discusses ways to overcome jQuery's reputation of being the source of difficult-to-read spaghetti code.

Chapter 9, Faster jQuery, looks at some simple techniques to speed up your jQuery code and ways to measure its performance.

Chapter 10, Benefitting from the Work of Others with Plugins, introduces the jQuery UI and plugins, both of which make it easier to enhance your site using code written by others.

What you need for this book

To follow the code used in this book, all you will need is a programmer's text editor. A full-blown Integrated Development Environment (IDE) can be used, but it is not required. Most of the examples will run directly in a browser, with the exception of those covering Ajax. In order to run the Ajax examples, you'll need a web server or an IDE with a built-in server.

Who this book is for

Whether you are a beginner or an experienced developer who is looking for quick answers, you will find what you need in this book.

Conventions

In this book, you will find a number of text styles that distinguish between different kinds of information. Here are some examples of these styles and an explanation of their meaning.

Code words in text, database table names, folder names, filenames, file extensions, pathnames, dummy URLs, user input, and Twitter handles are shown as follows: "The document methods return different things depending on which method you call. If you call `document.getElementById`, it returns either an element object or `null` if the element is not found."

A block of code is set as follows:

```
var $hide = $('#hide'),
      $show = $('#show'),
      $toggle = $('#toggle'),
      $allPictures = $('#allPictures')
```

When we wish to draw your attention to a particular part of a code block, the relevant lines or items are set in bold:

```
$(document).ready(function () {
    var $hide = $('#hide'),
        $show = $('#show'),
        $toggle = $('#toggle'),
        $allPictures = $('#allPictures');

    $hide.click(function () {
        $allPictures.hide();
    });
    $show.click(function () {
        $allPictures.show();
    });
    $toggle.click(function () {
        $allPictures.toggle();
    });
});
```

New terms and **important words** are shown in bold. Words that you see on the screen, for example, in menus or dialog boxes, appear in the text like this: "The user interface consists of a single button labeled **stop** and a horizontal rule. Members will appear below the horizontal rule, and messages will appear next to the button."

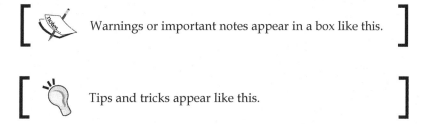

[Warnings or important notes appear in a box like this.]

[Tips and tricks appear like this.]

Reader feedback

Feedback from our readers is always welcome. Let us know what you think about this book—what you liked or disliked. Reader feedback is important for us as it helps us develop titles that you will really get the most out of.

To send us general feedback, simply e-mail feedback@packtpub.com, and mention the book's title in the subject of your message.

If there is a topic that you have expertise in and you are interested in either writing or contributing to a book, see our author guide at www.packtpub.com/authors.

Customer support

Now that you are the proud owner of a Packt book, we have a number of things to help you to get the most from your purchase.

Downloading the example code

You can download the example code files from your account at http://www.packtpub.com for all the Packt Publishing books you have purchased. If you purchased this book elsewhere, you can visit http://www.packtpub.com/support and register to have the files e-mailed directly to you.

Errata

Although we have taken every care to ensure the accuracy of our content, mistakes do happen. If you find a mistake in one of our books—maybe a mistake in the text or the code—we would be grateful if you could report this to us. By doing so, you can save other readers from frustration and help us improve subsequent versions of this book. If you find any errata, please report them by visiting http://www.packtpub.com/submit-errata, selecting your book, clicking on the **Errata Submission Form** link, and entering the details of your errata. Once your errata are verified, your submission will be accepted and the errata will be uploaded to our website or added to any list of existing errata under the Errata section of that title.

To view the previously submitted errata, go to https://www.packtpub.com/books/content/support and enter the name of the book in the search field. The required information will appear under the **Errata** section.

Piracy

Piracy of copyrighted material on the Internet is an ongoing problem across all media. At Packt, we take the protection of our copyright and licenses very seriously. If you come across any illegal copies of our works in any form on the Internet, please provide us with the location address or website name immediately so that we can pursue a remedy.

Please contact us at `copyright@packtpub.com` with a link to the suspected pirated material.

We appreciate your help in protecting our authors and our ability to bring you valuable content.

Questions

If you have a problem with any aspect of this book, you can contact us at `questions@packtpub.com`, and we will do our best to address the problem.

1
jQuery Part by Part

jQuery is hands down the most popular JavaScript library on the Internet. According to `http://builtwith.com`, it is used by over 87% of the websites that use a JavaScript library. That is an amazing amount of penetration. It is hard to believe that jQuery has only been around since 2006.

In this chapter, we will start to get you familiar with jQuery. We will cover the following topics:

- Why was jQuery created?
- The major components of jQuery
- Why are there two maintained versions of jQuery?
- What is a content delivery network?

Life before jQuery

2006 may not seem that long ago, but it is almost a lifetime in Internet years. If you don't agree, think about what kind of cellphone you had then, if you had one. At that time, the four most popular browsers were Internet Explorer, Firefox, Safari, and Opera. What about Chrome? It didn't exist yet, and it wouldn't come along until late 2008. Internet Explorer, used by over 80% of users, was by far the most popular.

At that time, Microsoft didn't seem too concerned with being standards-compliant. Why should they? They had over 80% of the market. If a website had to choose, they usually chose to work with IE. But the winds of change were already blowing. 80% might seem like an insurmountable lead, but two years ago, it was over 90%. The other browsers, led by Firefox, were slowly but surely chipping away at that lead. Lots of people, including developers, were switching to alternative browsers and they wanted websites that worked on them.

Unfortunately, writing web applications is tough now and it was worse then. JavaScript is not the friendliest programming language around. But JavaScript was not the problem; browsers were the problem. The same code ran on different browsers and behaved differently. On one, it ran perfectly; on another, it crashed, leaving users frustrated.

To understand how differences in browser implementations could result in lots of extra work for developers, let's take a look at implementing a JavaScript Ajax call. In 2006, the **W3C (World Wide Web Consortium)** standards didn't cover the XMLHttpRequest object that lies at the heart of all Ajax requests. Microsoft invented the technology way back in 1999 with Internet Explorer version 5. Unfortunately, they chose to implement it as an ActiveX control. ActiveX was a proprietary Microsoft technology, so there was no way other browsers could implement it in the same way. Mozilla, Safari, and Opera chose to implement it as an object attached to the global window. So, in order to add Ajax to a website that could work on all browsers, developers had to write, test, and maintain twice as much code as they should: a set of code for IE and another set of code for everybody else.

Are you thinking how hard could it be to detect whether the browser was IE and do something different? Well, you are right it isn't that hard to detect which browser your code is running, but it is hard to do it reliably because browsers can lie. According to the W3C standard, the way to detect the browser is simple:

```
window.navigator.appName
```

This property is supposed to return the name of the browser, but if you try it on Chrome, Safari, or Internet Explorer, they all return the same value, "Netscape". What gives? As I already said, browsers can lie.

Downloading the example code

You can download the example code files from your account at http://www.packtpub.com for all the Packt Publishing books you have purchased. If you purchased this book elsewhere, you can visit http://www.packtpub.com/support and register to have the files e-mailed directly to you.

During the 90s, websites began to detect which browsers were visiting them. At that time, there were really only three browsers: Netscape Navigator, Microsoft's Internet Explorer and the browser that started it all, NCSA Mosaic. Mosaic was created by the National Center for Supercomputing Applications at the University of Illinois Urbana-Champaign. At this time, the real battle for browser supremacy raged between Microsoft and Netscape. The companies fought by adding new features to their browsers.

One of the features that Netscape added to their browser was the frame element. It was very popular. Many websites of the time would only use the frame element if the browser was Netscape Navigator. They checked for Netscape either using `window.navigator.appName` or by `window.navigator.userAgent`. Navigator's code name was Mozilla, which was included in the user agent string. Later, when Microsoft added the frame element to IE, websites continued to not serve frame-based content to IE since they only identify the browser by name, not by feature detection. So, IE began to lie. It returned Netscape from `window.navigator.appName` and included Mozilla in its user agent. Now, for historical compatibility, many other browsers lie too.

There are two ways to deal with browser compatibility issues. The first way is the one we've already shown: browser detection. Browser detection is tougher than you think, and it can have unintended side effects, just like the failure of websites to serve frames to IE even after it supported them. The second technique is feature detection, also known as property sniffing. Before you use a feature, you should make sure the browser supports it. While this is usually more difficult code to write, it is much more beneficial to users. If the feature isn't supported in one version of a browser, it may be supported in the next. Feature detection is the method used in jQuery.

Best practice

Use feature detection, not browser detection. If you need to write code to detect a feature yourself instead of using jQuery or some other third-party solution such as Modernizr, always use feature detection and never use browser detection.

Why was jQuery created?

One of the major reasons for the creation of jQuery was to free developers from having to check the entire myriad of features, which were implemented differently on the available browsers. In fact, jQuery's motto is "write less, do more". One of the goals of jQuery is to free developers from writing plumbing code and concentrate on adding functionalities to their websites instead.

The major components of jQuery

Looking at the jQuery API page, `http://api.jquery.com`, for the first time can be mind-numbing. It lists over 300 different methods. Don't freak out; there is a method to the madness. Most of the API methods can be divided into just a few categories.

The DOM selection

These are the methods that give jQuery its name. They help find the element or elements that you are looking for in the **document object model** (**DOM**). If you know browser JavaScript, you are probably thinking what is the big deal? It has always been possible to query the DOM. There are `document.getElementById`, `document.getElementsByClassName`, and so on. But the interface of jQuery is much cleaner than any of these methods. jQuery uses CSS-style selectors to parse the DOM, and it consistently returns a jQuery object as an array of zero or more elements.

The document methods return different things depending on which method you call. If you call `document.getElementById`, it returns either an element object or null if the element is not found. For `document.getElementsByClassName`, it returns `HTMLCollection`, an array-like object.

DOM manipulation

Once you have found an element, you will usually want to modify it somehow. jQuery has an extensive set of manipulation methods. The built-in document methods can't compare. jQuery's methods allow you to delete or replace markups. You can also insert a new markup before, after, or surrounding the old markup.

Events

Being able to handle events is crucial to creating a dynamic website. While modern browsers all pretty much follow the standards, this wasn't the case a few years ago. jQuery makes it possible to support both modern and old browsers from the same code base.

Form

A good number of websites on the Internet have one or more forums to send user information back to a web server. These methods make it easier to send the information back to a server.

CSS and animation

CSS methods are convenience methods and aid the handling of classes and the locations and dimensions of elements. Unlike the built-in JavaScript methods, they do far more than simply reading the class attributes' string; they allow you to add, remove, toggle, and check for the presence of a class.

Animation methods are simple but add polish to your website. No longer do you have to settle for a markup, which appears or disappears; now, it fades in or out or even slides in or out. And if you are so inclined, you can use jQuery's effect framework to create your own custom animation effects.

Ajax

As we've already discussed, Ajax is one of the main features of jQuery. Even if you don't need to support legacy browsers, jQuery's Ajax methods are much cleaner than those of the browser. They also have built-in support for asynchronous success and error functions and even return a JavaScript promise object.

Helpers

The final, main group of jQuery methods is about helper functions, such as `.each()`, to iterate over a collection. jQuery also adds methods to determine the type of a JavaScript object, and it functions strangely missing from the language. Plus, it adds other methods that don't fit neatly into a category.

Why are there two maintained versions of jQuery?

After nearly 7 years of development, jQuery was beginning to show its age. The 1.8 version was a major release and included a rewrite of the Sizzle Selector Engine and improvements to the animations, but more was needed. There were some inconsistencies in the interface, there were lots of deprecated methods, and there was lots of code in need of thorough cleaning. So, the version 1.9 release consisted of jQuery and the jQuery Migrate plugin.

The jQuery development team believed 1.9 was such a huge change that they created the jQuery Migrate plugin to help ease the transition. The Migrate plugin included all of the deprecated methods, which sounds weird, but in its development version, it console logged the use of deprecated methods. This gave developers a working site and a way to know what things needed to be fixed. The production version doesn't do any extra logging.

The 2.0 version came out a few months later, and it brought a friend. The development team, continuing to address both the platform's weight and speed, decided to drop support for all versions of Internet Explorer below 9. A great deal of code in jQuery was written specifically for the quirks in older versions of Internet Explorer. The difference was dramatic. The minimized version of jQuery 1.10 is 93 KB, while the minimized version of jQuery 2.0 clocks in at 83 KB, a nearly an 11% reduction in size.

So, for now and the foreseeable future, there will be two versions of jQuery: the 1.x version that supports most browsers, including Internet Explorer versions 6, 7, and 8. The 2.x version supports all modern browsers, including IE versions 9 and higher. It is important to note that both versions have the same API, though their internals are different.

The difference between minified and un-minified versions

For each branch of jQuery, there are two versions: minified and un-minified. The un-minified version is intended only for development. It allows you to easily step through jQuery code while debugging and gives more meaningful stack traces. The minified version should be used in production. It has undergone minification, which removes all of the unnecessary whitespace and renames of JavaScript variables and internal methods. Minification decreases the download time of the file. The development version of jQuery 2.1.1 is 247 KB, while the production version is only 84 KB.

Should the need ever arise to debug the minified version of jQuery, you can download the source map file. A source map allows you to have access to the original debug information and is supported by all modern browsers, including IE.

What is a content delivery network?

The faster your site loads, the more visitors are encouraged to return later. Another way to speed up your load time is to use a **content delivery network**, or **CDN**. The magic of a CDN is twofold. First, CDNs are usually located on edge servers, which means that rather than being hosted at a single physical location, they are located at multiple locations across the Internet. This means they can be found and downloaded faster. Second, browsers will usually cache static files on the user's machine, and loading a local file is orders of magnitude faster than downloading it from the Internet. CDNs are used by lots of companies, big and small. So, it is possible that one of them is using the same copy of jQuery that your site needs and has already cached it locally on the user's machine. So, when your site asks for it, voila, it is already there, and your site gets a nice performance boost for free.

Summary

Modern browsers are far more capable than their nearly forgotten ancestors. It would be easy for a new web developer to wonder why jQuery exists. In this chapter, we explored the reasons for its existence by taking a look at what web development was like before jQuery. We then broke jQuery's API into easy-to-digest major components. We learned why it makes sense for jQuery to have two maintained versions and why each version has two different forms. In the next chapter, we will start digging into the API and learn how to write selectors and filters.

2
jQuery Selectors and Filters

The name "jQuery" comes from the library's ability to quickly and intelligently query the **DOM (Document Object Model)**.

In this chapter, we will learn how to query the DOM ourselves and, once we have a set of items, how to use filters to further refine our dataset. We will cover the following topics:

- What selectors and filters are
- How to create a selector
- How to create a filter
- How to query based on element attributes
- How chaining allows us to quickly and neatly continue queries

jQuery selectors

Underneath every browser web page is the DOM. The DOM keeps track of all the individual objects that are rendered to the page. Being able to find DOM elements is the first step toward creating a dynamic web page. The browser comes with built-in methods to query the DOM. These methods usually begin with the word `document`. There is `document.getElementById`, `document.getElementsByClass`, and so on. The problem with these methods is that their interface is neither consistent nor complete.

jQuery gets its name from its ability to query the DOM. Unlike browser methods, its interface is both complete and feature-rich. Querying the DOM begins by creating a selector. A selector is a string that tells jQuery how to find the elements you want. Since it is a string of text, the possible number of selectors is limitless. But don't panic; they all fall into a few broad classes.

The chapter code

The code for this chapter is contained in a directory named `chapter02`. Keep in mind that this is sample code meant to teach, and it is not intended for production. The code does two things that are particularly tedious and worth mentioning. First, it uses inline JavaScript, which means that the JavaScript is contained in a script tag with the main page's HTML. This violates the rule of separation of concerns and can lead to poorly performing code. Second, it makes heavy use of alerts. The browser `alert` method is a quick and dirty way to display something on a screen, and unlike the `console.log` method, all browsers support it. But it is not recommended for use in production. Alerts can't be styled, so they will stick out like a sore thumb unless your website is not styled as well. Second, alerts cause the browser to stop everything and force the user to acknowledge them, which is obviously something that can quickly become annoying to the user:

```
function showJqueryObject(title, $ptr) {
    var ndx, sb = title + "\n";

    if ($ptr) {
        for (ndx = 0; ndx < $ptr.length; ndx += 1) {
            sb += $ptr[ndx].outerHTML + "\n";
        }
        alert(sb);
    }
}
```

The method used to display the jQuery object is named `showJqueryObject()`. It iterates through the jQuery object, showing each of the nodes in turn. Now, to be perfectly honest, I only use this method for the purpose of this book. When working on issues while developing my own programs, I normally rely on the browser's `console.log` method. But since not all browsers support it, and for those that support it differently, the easiest way to display something on the screen is to roll my own method.

Protocol-relative URLs

A curious thing that keen-eyed readers might notice is that the protocol is missing from the URL in the script tag. I am not a web security expert, but I am smart enough to pay heed to the warnings of web security experts, all of whom will say that mixing HTTP protocols is dangerous. Protocol-relative URLs make it easy to keep your site secure. These days, many sites will run on either open HTTP or secured HTTP (HTTPS). Achieving this feat previously required loading all JavaScript libraries from your own site, foregoing the benefits of CDNs, or including some complicated bit of inline JavaScript that detects your site's protocol and uses `document.write` to inject some new JavaScript onto the page.

With protocol-relative URLs, you simply omit the protocol from the URL. Then when your site is loaded, if it is loaded from HTTP, the libraries will also be loaded from HTTP. If it is loaded via HTTPS, then all of the libraries will also be loaded via HTTPS.

The jQuery object

Before we take a look at the classes of jQuery selectors, let's first look at what gets returned by the selector. The result of a call to a selector is always a jQuery object. A jQuery object has a lot of array-like features, but it is not an array. If you use the jQuery `isArray()` function on it, it will return false. For many things, the difference doesn't matter, but occasionally, you may want to execute something like `concat()`, but unfortunately, this array method doesn't exist on a jQuery object though it has a nearly equivalent method, `add()`.

If no elements matching the selector are found, then the length of the jQuery object is zero. The null value is never returned. The result is a jQuery object with a length of zero or more. This is an important thing to understand since it reduces the amount of work you need to do when checking the results of a jQuery call. You only have to check whether the length is greater than zero.

When making a call to jQuery, you can use its formal name, `jQuery`, or its shortened name, '`$`'. Also, keep in mind that strings in JavaScript can begin with either a single or double quote just so long as they end with the same quotation mark. So, in the examples, you may see either single or double quotes, and there is usually no rhyme or reason why I chose one over the other.

> One of the interesting things about JavaScript in the browser is that some methods are not actually part of JavaScript; instead, they are provided by the browser. This becomes clear when you use JavaScript in an environment that is not browser-based, such as `node.js`. The methods of the document method, for example, are not part of JavaScript; they are part of the browser. In `node.js`, there is no document object and hence no document method. Two other sources of browser methods are window and navigator objects.

Creating selectors

One of the things that makes jQuery selectors so cool and easy to learn is that they are based on the selectors used by CSS; this is not the case with the browser methods. So, if you already know how to create CSS selectors, you will have no trouble learning about jQuery selectors. If you don't know about CSS selectors, don't worry; jQuery selectors are still easy to learn, and knowing about them will give you a head start on learning about CSS selectors.

ID selectors

The first kind of selector we will look at is the ID selector. It begins with a hash sign and is followed by the same string used in the ID attribute of the desired element. Take a look at this example:

```
<div id="my-element"></div>
var jqObject = $("#my-element");
or
var jqObject = jQuery('#my-element');
```

From the preceding example, note that the result of the selector call is a jQuery object. We are free to use either style of quote marks. Also, we can make the call using either the formal name or the shortened one. For the remainder of this book, I will use the short name, $. The ID selector returns an array that contains either zero or one element. It will never return more than one element.

According to the **W3C (World Wide Web Consortium)** specification, each DOM element can have one ID selector at most, and each ID selector must be unique to the web page. Now, I've seen a lot of websites that violate the uniqueness rule. These are bad sites; don't emulate them. Also, they have unpredictable code. When more than one element with the same ID exists, only one will be returned, but there is no specification that says which one should be returned. So, code may behave differently depending on which browser it is run on.

Class selectors

The next type of selector that we will examine is the class selector. The class selector begins with a period and is followed by the name of a class that all of desired elements have. Unlike the ID selector that will return one element at most, the class selector can return zero, one, or more elements.

The order of the class in the element makes no difference. It can be the first, the last, or some class in the middle, and jQuery will find it:

```
var jqClassObject = $('.active');
```

Tag selectors

Sometimes, your desired elements don't have an ID or a class name; they simply have the same tag name. This is when you will use the tag selector. It searches for elements with a specific tag name, such as `div`, `p`, `li`, and so on. To create a tag selector, you pass the name of the tag surrounded by quote marks:

```
var jqTagObject = $('div');
```

Combining selectors

What should we do if we want all of the paragraph tags in a single set on the page and all elements that contain the `active` class? We could make two calls and then use the jQuery `add` method to add the resulting objects together. A better way is to combine the selectors and let jQuery do the grunt work of combining the results together. To combine selectors, simply put two or more selectors together in the string and separate them with a comma:

```
        var jqClassResults = $('.special'),
            jqTagResults = $('p'),
            jqTotal = jqClassResults.add(jqTagResults);

    var jqTotal = $('.special, p'); // give me all of the elements with
    the special class and all of the paragraphs
```

It is important to remember that a comma is used to separate the selectors. If you forget the comma, you won't get an error; you will get a result, only not the result you were expecting. Instead, it will be the end result of a descendent selector, which is something we will cover in just a bit.

Descendent selectors

Sometimes, the elements you want don't have an easy-to-design selector. Maybe they are all children or grandchildren of a specific element. This is where descendent selectors come in. They allow you to narrow the focus of the query to a specific ancestor and then query from there. There are two types of descendent selectors: child selectors and descendant selectors. The desired child must be a direct child of the parent. To create a child selector, you create the parent selector, add a greater than symbol, and then add the selector to find the children from within the result of the parent's results set.

Consider the following HTML markup:

```
<ul id="languages">
    <li>Mandarin</li>
    <li>English
        <ul class="greetings">
            <li class="main-greeting">Hi</li>
            <li>Hello</li>
            <li>Slang
                <ul data-troy>
                    <li>What's up doc?</li>
                </ul>
            </li>
        </ul>
    </li>
    <li>Hindustani</li>
    <li data-troy="true">Spanish</li>
    <li>Russian</li>
    <li>Arabic</li>
    <li>Bengali</li>
    <li>Portuguese</li>
    <li>Malay-Indonesian</li>
    <li>French</li>
</ul>
```

Take a look at the following code as well:

```
var jqChildren = $('#languages>li');
showJqueryObject("Direct", jqChildren);
```

The preceding code sample will return all of the `<li>` tags that are children of the `<ul id="languages">` element. It will not return the `<li>` tags that are children of the `<ul class="greetings">` tag because these are its grandchildren:

```
var jqDescendant = $('#languages li');
showJqueryObject("Direct", jqDescendant);
```

A descendant selector is nearly identical to a child selector except that it lacks the greater than sign. The second query will return all of the `<li>` tags contained in `<ul id="languages">` regardless of how far down the descendant tree they are.

Attribute selectors

In addition to selecting elements based on their basic characteristics, such as the name, tag, and classes, we can also select elements based on their attributes. Attribute selectors are a bit tricky to work with because their syntax is more complicated. Also, keep in mind that like other jQuery selectors, if you get the syntax wrong, you will not get an error; you will simply get a jQuery object of zero length.

There are only nine attribute selectors, so they are fairly easy to remember, and they are as follows:

- The `Has Attribute` selector
- The `Attribute Equals` selector
- The `Attribute Not Equal` selector
- The `Attribute Contains` selector
- The `Attribute Starts With` selector
- The `Attribute Ends With` selector
- The `Attribute Contains Prefix` selector
- The `Attribute Contains Word` selector
- The `Multiple Attribute` selector

Let's begin with the simplest one: the `Has Attribute` selector. This selects all of the elements that have the specified attribute. The value of the attribute doesn't matter; in fact, it doesn't even have to have a value:

```
var jqHasAttr = $("[name]");
```

As far as selectors go, this one is very simple. It consists of the name of the desired attribute surrounded by square braces. The next two selectors are only slightly more complicated.

The `Has Attribute` selector doesn't care about the attribute's value, but sometimes, you need the attribute to either have or not have a specific value. This is where the `Attribute Equals` selector and its opposite, the `Attribute Not Equals` selector, come in. The former returns all of the elements that have both the desired attribute and the desired value. Keep in mind that this must be an exact match; something close won't count. The latter returns all of the elements that either don't have the desired attribute or have it but don't have the desired value. The `Attribute Not Equals` selector returns all of the elements that weren't returned by the `Attribute Equals` selector. This is confusing to people sometimes, but it shouldn't be. Just remember that these two selectors are opposites:

```
var jqEqualAttr = $('[data-employee="Bob"]');

var jqNotEqualAttr = $('[data-employee!="Bob"]');
```

The next three selectors are also related to each other. Each looks for an attribute with a value, only now the value is a substring instead of an exact match. The thing that differentiates the three is where they look for the substring. The first one, the `Attribute Contains` selector looks for a substring anywhere in the attribute's value. So as long as the string is contained with the value, it passes:

```
var jqContainsAttr = $('[data-employee*="Bob"]');
showJqueryObject("Contains Attribute", jqContainsAttr);
```

The `Attribute Starts With` selector is more specific about where the specified substring is located. With it, the string must be at the beginning of the value. The value string doesn't have to be a complete match; only the beginning of the strings must match:

```
var jqStartsAttr = $('[data-employee^="Bob"]');
showJqueryObject("Starts Attribute", jqStartsAttr);
```

The `Attribute Ends With` selector matches the specified string to the end of the value string. If the end of the value string matches the specified string, all is good. Just like with the `Attribute Starts With` selector, the rest of the string doesn't have to match:

```
var jqEndsAttr = $('[data-employee$="Bob"]');
showJqueryObject("Ends Attribute", jqEndsAttr);
```

Telling these selectors apart can be a bit of a pain since they only vary by one character, but if you know JavaScript regular expressions, you will recognize that jQuery borrowed from them. The '^' in a regular expression refers to the beginning of a string, and it is used by the `Attribute Begins With` selector. The '$' in a regular expression refers to the end of a string, and it used in the `Attribute Ends With` selector. The `Attribute Contains` selector uses the asterisk, *, which is the regular expression wildcard character.

The `Attribute Contains Prefix` selector looks for the specified string at the beginning of the value string. It differs from the `Attribute Begins With` selector in that the string must match the value exactly if there is no hyphen. If there is a hyphen in the value, then the string needs to match the hyphen.

The `Attribute Contains Word` selector checks for the specified string anywhere in the value string. This may sound suspiciously like the `Attribute Contains` selector, but there is a subtle difference. The specified string must be surrounded by whitespace, whereas the `Attribute Contains` selector doesn't care where the string is or what is delimiting it:

```
Attribute Contains Word Selector [name~="value"]
```

The final attribute selector is the `Multiple Attribute` selector, which is just a combination of any of the previous attribute selectors. Each selector is contained within its own square brackets and is concatenated together. There is no need for any separation character:

```
Multiple Attribute Selector [name="value"][name2="value2"]
```

Now that we have learned some ways to select elements, let's learn how to filter the result set of our selection.

Creating basic filter selectors

Filters take the results of a selector call and whittle it down some more. There are three types of filter selectors: basic, child, and content. Basic selectors just operate on the jQuery object result set. Child selectors operate on the parent-child relation between elements. And the content filters work on the contents of each of the elements of the result set.

There are 14 basic filter selectors. The first group deals with the position of a result in the result set. Let's deal with them first.

One of the easiest to understand is the `:eq()` filter selector. It retrieves the result when the index number is passed. It is very much like accessing an element in a JavaScript array. And like an array, it is zero-based, so the first element is zero, not one:

```
var jqEq = $("a:eq(1)");
showJqueryObject("EQ Attribute", jqEq);
```

You create an `:eq()` filter selector by adding a colon and `eq(x)` to a regular selector. The x here refers to the element's index. If your index is out of bounds, no error will be generated.

The `:eq()` filter selector allows you to access any item in the result set as long as you know the range of possible indexes. But sometimes, this is too much work. You may only want to know the first or the last element. For these occasions, jQuery provides the `:first` and `:last` filter selectors. Each does exactly as their name says: it gets the first or last element:

```
var jqFirst = $("a:first");
showJqueryObject("First Attribute", jqFirst);
var jqLast = $("a:last");
showJqueryObject("Last Attribute", jqLast);
```

Sticking with the theme of index operations, there are times when we want all of the elements up to a certain index or all of those with an index greater than a number. For these times, there are the :lt() and :gt() selectors. The :lt() selectors return all of the elements whose index is less than the passed value. The :gt() selectors return all of the elements that are greater than it. Both of these selectors also accept negative values, which count from the end of the result set rather than the start:

```
var jqLt = $("a:lt(1)");
showJqueryObject("Less Than Selector", jqLt);
var jqGt = $("a:gt(1)");
showJqueryObject("Greater Than Attribute", jqGt);
jqLt = $("a:lt(-4)");
showJqueryObject("Less Than Selector", jqLt);
jqGt = $("a:gt(-2)");
showJqueryObject("Greater Than Attribute", jqGt);
```

The final two of the basic filters are super handy. They are the :even and :odd selectors. They are pretty simple except for one small weirdness. JavaScript is zero-based, so 0 is the first element and zero is even, which means that the even selector will grab the first, third, fifth (and so on) elements. Also, the odd selector will get the second, fourth, sixth (and so on) elements. It seems weird, but it makes perfect sense as long as you remember that JavaScript is zero-based.

The remaining basic attribute filters don't fit neatly into any category. So, we will just walk through them one by one, beginning with the :animated selector. The :animated selector returns all of the elements that are currently performing animation. Keep in mind that it won't autoupdate, so the state of things that were there at the time the query was run, but things will change afterwards.

The :focus selector returns the currently selected element if it is in the current result set. Be careful with this selector. I will deal with performance issues in a later chapter, but this one can have extremely poor performance if it is not used with a result set. Consider that you simply make the following call:

```
var jqFocus = $(":focus");
showJqueryObject("The Focused Element", jqFocus);
```

It will search the entire DOM tree for the focused element, which may or may not exist. While the preceding call will work, there are much faster ways to do this.

The `:header` selector is a handy utility method that returns all of the elements, which are `<h1>`, `<h2>`, `<h3>`, `<h4>`, `<h5>`, and `<h6>`. It would be pretty easy to make an equivalent to this method yourself, but why bother when this shortcut is readily at hand:

```
var jqHeader = $(":header");
showJqueryObject("The Header Elements", jqHeader);
```

The `:lang` selector will find all of the elements that match the specified language. It will match either the language code by itself, en, or the language code paired with the country code, en-us. With the increased emphasis on creating global websites, this selector grows more important everyday:

```
var jqLang = $("a:lang('en')");
showJqueryObject("The Lang Elements", jqLang);
```

The `:not` selector is not one of my favorite selectors. It does a logical `not` operation on the passed selectors.

It has been around since the beginning of jQuery, but in my humble opinion, it leads to confusing code. And the last thing that jQuery needs is even hard-to-read code. I will talk more about writing readable jQuery code in *Chapter 6, Better Forms with jQuery*, but for now, you should avoid this one if you can:

```
var jqNot = $( "a:not(:lang('en'))");
showJqueryObject("The Not Elements", jqNot);
```

The `:target` selector sounds complicated, but given the abundance of single page JavaScript apps, it can be very useful. It looks at the URL of the current page. If it has a fragment, which is identified with a hash sign, it will match the element whose ID matches that fragment. This is one of the more recent additions to jQuery, having been added with the 1.9 version.

And finally, let's talk about the `:root` selector. I will be honest and admit I haven't needed to use this one yet. It returns the root element of the document, which is always the `<html>` element in HTML:

```
var jqRoot = $( ":root");
alert("The Root Element: " + jqRoot.get(0).tagName);
```

Content filters

There are only four content filter selectors. I will give a general word of caution with all of these selectors since they can be performance-challenged. I will go into more details on performance in *Chapter 7, Talking to Your Server*, but until then use these selectors only if you must.

The first two of these selectors, :empty and :parent, are inverses of each other. The first one, the :empty selector, returns all of the elements that have no children. The second one, the :parent selector, selects all the elements that have at least one child.

The :contains selector returns all of the elements that have the specified string. The case of the strings must match. The string can be on any descendent.

The :has() selector selects all the elements that contain at least one match for the specified selector.

Next, there are child selectors. These all deal with the parent-child relationship between elements. The first group is pretty easy to understand; it deals with the position of the child among all of the children. All of the example code will reference the following markup:

```html
<div>
    <p>I am the first child of div #1.</p>
    <p>I am the second child of div #1.</p>
    <p>I am the third child of div #1.</p>
    <p>I am the fourth child of div #1.</p>
    <p>I am the fifth child of div #1.</p>
</div>
<div>
    <p>I am the first child of div #2.</p>
    <p>I am the second child of div #2.</p>
    <p>I am the third child of div #2.</p>
</div>
<div>
    <p>I am the only child of div #3.</p>
</div>
```

First up is the :first-child selector; it selects all of the elements that are the first child of their parent. Unlike the :first selector, it can return multiple elements:

```javascript
var jqChild = $('div p:first-child');
showJqueryObject("First Child", jqChild);
```

The first line of the example code says that you should grab all of the paragraph descendants of the div tags. There are three defined <div> tags; the first one has five paragraphs, the second one has three paragraphs, and the third one has only one paragraph. The :first-child selector looks at those nine paragraphs and finds the three that are the first children of their respective parents. Here they are:

```
<p>I am the first child of div #1.</p>
<p>I am the first child of div #2.</p>
<p>I am the only child of div #3.</p>
```

The :last-child selector operates in a manner similar to first-child except that it searches for the last child of their respective parent:

```
var jqLastChild = $('div p:last-child');
showJqueryObject("Last Child", jqLastChild);
```

Again, we are asking for all of the paragraph children of the div tags and then filtering the return set with the child selector. This example is nearly identical to the previous, except that the elements returned by it are counted from the end, not the beginning:

```
<p>I am the fifth child of div #1.</p>
<p>I am the third child of div #2.</p>
<p>I am the only child of div #3.</p>
```

If you did a double-take on the fact that the last paragraph, <p>I am the only child of div #3.</p>, is identical for both method calls, don't be alarmed. Remember, it is the only child of the third <div>, so it is both the first and the last child.

Next, we have the :nth-child() selector. It returns the children whose index is passed to the method. The first-child selector can be thought of as a special case of this selector where the passed index is 1. As I've mentioned previously, if you pass an index value that is out of range, there is no error; you simply get a jQuery object of a length that equals 0:

```
var jqNthChild = $('div p:nth-child(2)');
showJqueryObject("Nth Child", jqNthChild);
```

A special thing about this and the :nth-last-child() selectors is that in addition to passing an index value, you can also pass in some special values. The first two special values are even and odd. These will return the even and the odd children of their respective parents. The result set is different from that of the :even selector. Because these selectors are based on CSS, counting begins with one, not the zero of JavaScript. So, take a look at the following code:

```
var jqNthChild = $('div p:nth-child(odd)');
showJqueryObject("Nth Child", jqNthChild);
```

The odd parameter will return the first, third, fifth (and so forth) elements:

```
<p>I am the first child of div #1.</p>
<p>I am the third child of div #1.</p>
<p>I am the fifth child of div #1.</p>
<p>I am the first child of div #2.</p>
<p>I am the third child of div #2.</p>
```

The `:nth-last-child()` selector is essentially the same as the `nth-child()` selector except that it counts backwards from the end of the list instead of the beginning. The `:last-child` selector can, likewise, be thought of as a special case of this selector with a passed index of 1. And like the `:nth-child` selector, it can accept the special parameters of even, odd, or a formula:

```
var jqNthLastChild = $('div p:nth-last-child(3)');
showJqueryObject("Nth Last Child", jqNthLastChild);
```

The result set from the example code consists of two elements, the third child from the end of their respective parents:

```
<p>I am the third child of div #1.</p>
<p>I am the first child of div #2.</p>
```

The last of the child selectors is `:only-child`. It returns the elements that only children of their respective parents can:

```
var jqOnlyChild = $('div p:only-child');
showJqueryObject("Only Child", jqOnlyChild);
```

Since there is only one paragraph that is an only child, the following element is displayed:

```
<p>I am the only child of div #3.</p>
```

The next selectors are the `of-type` selectors. All of these selectors work on siblings of the same element type. The first of these is the `:first-of-type` selector, which will return the first element of the type for each parent:

```
var jqFirstOfType = $('p:first-of-type');
showJqueryObject("First Of Type", jqFirstOfType);
```

The difference between the child selectors and the `of-type` selectors is subtle but important. The `of-type` selectors don't specify the parent element. You simply tell jQuery about the children, and it figures out which ones are siblings and who the parents are.

The :last-of-type selector does exactly what we should expect based on everything we've already learned about jQuery. It returns the last element of the type:

```
var jqLastOfType = $('p:last-of-type');
showJqueryObject("Last Of Type", jqLastOfType);
```

The last of the of-type selectors will seem familiar; it is the :only-of-type selector. Like the :only-child selector, it returns the only children. But unlike the :only-child selector, it looks at the type of the element. So, consider that we change the third <div> to the following:

```
<div>
    <p>I am the only child of div #3.</p>
    <span>Here is some text</span>
</div>
```

We make the change when we run the following code sample:

```
var jqOnlyOfType = $('p:only-of-type');
showJqueryObject("Only Of Type", jqOnlyOfType);
```

This returns the following element:

```
<p>I am the only child of div #3.</p>
```

However, the corresponding code written using the :only-child selector returns no elements:

```
var jqOnlyChild = $('div p:only-child');
showJqueryObject("Only Child", jqOnlyChild);
```

Using chaining to quickly and neatly continue queries

One of the nice things about jQuery is its ability to chain queries. Any method call that returns the jQuery object can be chained, which means that all you need to do is add a period and your next method call. Be careful since not all methods return the jQuery object. Some methods, such as .width(), return a value that can't be chained. Each method of the chain performs its operations on the result set of the previous method call. If you perform filter operations further down the chain, then the result set is reduced, and the chained methods will work on the reduced set and not the original.

The next example isn't the greatest, but hopefully, it will begin to demonstrate the power of chaining:

```
var jqLiUl = $("li").find("ul");
showJqueryObject("LL UL", jqLiUl);
```

In this example, we first ask for all of the `<li>` elements on the page. Then, with the results set in hand, we ask for all of the `<ul>` elements it contains. We can ask for this more succinctly with the following code:

```
var jqLiUl = $("li ul");
showJqueryObject("LL UL concise", jqLiUl);
```

The point here is that we used jQuery's chaining ability to perform more operations on the result set. Often, you will use chaining to perform different operations in each link in the chain. You might want to add a CSS class at one step, perform DOM manipulations on another, and so on. For the sake of clarity, try to keep all of the operations related, or you may end up writing code that can't be read easily.

Summary

In this chapter, we began to dig into jQuery, and hopefully, we found out that it isn't as hopelessly complicated as it looks from the outside. We also saw that jQuery makes a habit of using preexisting ways of doing things. For example, it uses CSS selectors and symbols similar to those used by JavaScript regular expressions. It also follows a regular pattern of breaking things down. Once you get used to these patterns, you can almost predict the existence of certain methods.

Now that we have learned how to read elements from the DOM, in the next chapter, we will learn how to write markups to the DOM and begin to make dynamic web pages.

Manipulating the DOM

3

In the previous chapter, we learned how to use jQuery's selectors to find elements that we are looking for in the DOM. In this chapter, we will use this knowledge to first find elements and then modify them. We will learn the different methods that jQuery provides in order to help make our websites both beautiful and dynamic.

jQuery has over three dozen methods that manipulate the DOM in some way, but don't let that number scare you. All of the methods are readily broken down into just four different categories: dimensions and positions, classes and styles, attributes and properties, and content. Like most things in jQuery, once you dive in, you will quickly see the pattern of how the different groups of methods are related.

Many of the methods operate in one of two modes: getter or setter. In the getter mode, the method retrieves or gets values from the element and returns them to the caller. In the setter mode, the caller passes values to the method so that it can modify the matched set of elements. I think we are now ready to begin with dimensions and positions.

Many of the methods have two forms that only differ in the order of the selector and the content. One version will be in the more traditional form, which is the selector and then the content form, and the other will be in the content and then the selector form. The main reason for having the order reversed is chaining. When a method returns a jQuery object that contains the content we need for the next method in the chain, being able to use the content-first version gives us a method we can use.

This chapter will cover a lot of material. Here are the topics we will delve into:

- Dimensions and positions
- Reading the size of the screen and elements
- Classes and styles
- The JSON object
- Attributes and properties
- Keeping images proportional
- Removing attributes and properties

Dimensions and positions

In web development, we usually tend to not want to deal with the specifics of element sizes, but occasionally, such information comes in handy. Before we get into the details of reading the size, you need to know a few things. First, only the size of the first element in the matched set is returned. Two, reading a size kills the jQuery chain, so you can't have any other methods after it. Finally, there is more than one way to read the size of an element. The kind of method you choose depends on what you want to know. Let's take reading the width as an example.

Examples

In the previous chapter, we began with an empty web page and added just enough HTML to explain what each method does. In the real world, we seldom get a blank canvas to work on. So in this chapter, we are going to use a more complete looking web page instead, and it will be based on the very popular Bootstrap Jumbotron template. Bootstrap is one of the most popular CSS frameworks around, and using it in our examples will help you get familiar with modern website designs since it is not too common to write all of your own CSS these days. We aren't going to talk much about Bootstrap or how it works, but there are lots of good books on it at the Packt Publishing website, including *Learning Bootstrap*.

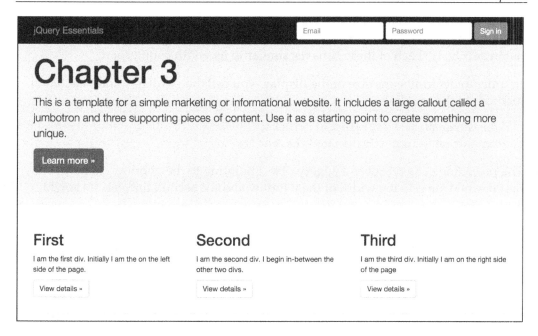

Developer tools

Most modern browsers have a built-in set of developer tools. How you activate the tools varies with the browser. In Internet Explorer, pressing *F12* activates the developer tools. In Chrome and Firefox, *Ctrl + Shift + I* does the job. We will be using the developer tools in order to see the console log output. By writing information to the log instead of displaying it using the `alert()` method, we won't break the flow of the site or annoy you with popups that you must respond to before being allowed to continue.

The console object of most modern browsers will have quite a few methods attached to it, but we are only concerned about one method, `log()`. We will use the `log()` method in its simplest form: to simply output strings. My hope is that the example code will run without any issue on any browser you run it on.

Reading the size of the screen and elements

There are three methods to read the width: `.width()`, `.innerWidth()`, and `.outerWidth()`. The first method, `.width()`, returns only the width of the element. The next method, `.innerWidth()`, returns the width of the element and its border and padding. The final method, `.outerWidth()`, returns the width of the element plus the border and padding, and if you pass true, it will also include the width of its margins.

For each method that deals with the elements' width, there is a matching method for the element's height. The methods are `.height()`, `.innerHeight()`, and `outerHeight()`. Each of these behaves similar to its width counterpart.

In order to determine the size of the display, you call the `.width()` and `.height()` methods of the window:

```
var screenWidth = $(window).width();
var screenHeight = $(window).height();
```

The preceding code retrieves a jQuery object pointing to the window element. The first line of code gets the width of the window and the second line gets its height.

Try not to get the window and the document confused. At times, they can give the same results, but keep in mind that the document can exceed the size of the window. When it does, scroll bars will appear. They are not equivalent.

Getting the dimensions of a screen element is nice, but sometimes, you need to know its position too. There is only one method that returns the position, and it is named `.position()`. Like the other value methods, it breaks the chain since it returns an object that contains the top and left values of the element's position relative to its parent.

There is a companion method to `.position()` called `.offset()`. The difference between them is important. The `.offset()` method returns the element's position relative to the document and not to its parent. Using the `.offset()` method allows us, for example, to compare two elements that have different parents, which is something that would be almost meaningless with the `.position()` method. We won't normally see the difference between the two methods unless we use either absolute or relative positioning instead of the browser default of static positioning:

```
// .position() vs. .offset()
var myPosition = $("body > .container > .row > .col-md-4:last").
position();
console.log("My Position = " + JSON.stringify(myPosition));
var myOffset = $("body > .container > .row > .col-md-4:last").
offset();
console.log("My Offset = " + JSON.stringify(myOffset));
```

The final two methods in this group are `.scrollLeft()` and `.scrollTop()`. These two methods are different from the rest since they are both getters and setters. If passed an argument, `.scrollLeft()` uses it to set the horizontal position of the scroll bar. The `.scrollTop()` method does something similar, setting the vertical position of the scroll bar. Both methods will set the position of every element in the matched set.

Classes and styles

The first method in the classes and styles group is `.css()`. This method is very powerful and shows why jQuery is a required and useful library even in the age of HTML5 browsers. The `.css()` method operates as both a getter and a setter. As a getter, it returns the computed style property or properties. It takes as arguments either a single string that is the name of a CSS property you would like to retrieve or an array of strings representing all of the CSS properties:

```
// .css(), retrieving a single property
var backgroundColor = $(".jumbotron > .container > p > a").
css("background-color");
console.log("Background Color = " + JSON.stringify(backgroundColor));
// .css(), retrieving multiple properties in a single call
var colors = $(".jumbotron > .container > p > a").css(["background-
color", "color"]);
console.log("Colors = " + JSON.stringify(colors));
```

The results of the preceding code are as follows:

Background Color = "rgb(51, 122, 183)"

Colors = {"background-color":"rgb(51, 122, 183)","color":"rgb(255, 255, 255)"}

The JSON object

Most modern browsers include the JSON object. JSON, like XML, is a data interchange format. It is language-independent, lightweight, and easy to understand. The JSON object added to browsers has two important methods. The first method, `.parse()`, takes a string representing a JSON object and converts it into a JavaScript object. The second function, `.stringify()`, takes a JavaScript object and converts it into a JSON string. These methods are intended to be used to serialize and deserialize objects. But we can also use the methods in our example code. The `.stringify()` method can render JavaScript objects as strings, and we can send these strings to the console.

One of the things that make the `.css()` method powerful is that it understands which properties you are referencing in a variety of different formats. Take, for example, the CSS property, `margin-left`. The DOM refers to it as `marginLeft`; jQuery understands both terms as the same thing. Likewise, it understands the browser method used to actually access properties with which most browsers call `getComputedStyle()`, but different versions of Internet Explorer call either `currentStyle()` or `runtimeStyle()`.

The setter mode of the `.css()` method has several ways to set properties. The first and easiest way is to simply pass in a property name and its new value as arguments:

```
// .css(), passing a property name and value, change the button to
orange
$(".jumbotron > .container > p > a").css("background-color",
"orange");
```

You can also remove a property in the same fashion by setting the value to an empty string. The next way in which we can change properties is to pass them in as key-value pairs in an object:

```
// .css(), passing in multiple properties as an object
var moreProperties =; { "background-color": "pink", "color": "black"};
$("body > .container > .row > .col-md-4 .btn:first").
css(moreProperties);
```

The final way in which we can change properties is by passing in a property and a function. The return value of the function is used by jQuery to set the property. If the function either doesn't return anything or returns "undefined," then no change is made to the property's value:

```
// .css(), setting a random background color on each call
$("body > .container > .row > .col-md-4 .btn:last").css("background-
color", function (index) {
    var r = Math.floor(Math.random() * 256),
            g = Math.floor(Math.random() * 256),
            b = Math.floor(Math.random() * 256),
            rgb = "rgb(" + r + "," + g + "," + b + ")";
    return rgb;
});
```

The preceding code snippet uses an anonymous function to set the background color of each of the selected elements. The function generates a random value for each of the colors and then places them into a string that is returned to the caller.

When you only have one or two properties that you are changing in one element, you can get away with directly tweaking the CSS properties of the element. But a better and faster way is to put all of the changes into CSS classes and add or remove a class to/from the elements. jQuery has four methods that will help you manipulate the classes assigned to an element.

The first method of this group is .addClass(), which adds a class to an element. If you assigned a class using the DOM methods, you will have to make sure that the class isn't being duplicated, but with .addClass(), if the class is already assigned to the element, it is not assigned twice. You aren't limited to assigning only one class at a time. You can add as many as you'd like just so long as you make sure that you separate each one with a space.

Like many other jQuery methods, .addClass() too has a really cool extra feature: it can accept a function as well. What's so cool about this? Well, imagine that you have a set of buttons and you would like to give each one a different color class depending on its place in the set. You can easily write a function to handle this scenario. jQuery passes two parameters to the function. The first is the index of the element in the matched set. The second parameter is a string that has all of the currently applied classes, each separated by a space. Here's an example:

```
// changes each of the buttons a different color
$("body > .container > .row > .col-md-4 .btn").addClass(function
(index) {
    var styles = ["info", "warning", "danger"],
            ndx = index % 3,
            newClass = "btn-" + styles[ndx];

    return newClass;
});
```

Eventually, we are going to need to delete a class, which is why we use .removeClass(). Depending on the parameters you pass to it, its behavior changes. If you pass a single class name to it, it removes that class. If you pass multiple class names separated by spaces, it removes those classes. And if you pass no arguments, it removes all of the currently assigned classes. If a passed class name doesn't exist, there is no error.

Like .addClass(), .removeClass() can also accept a function. jQuery passes an index to your function and all of the currently assigned classes as a string. To remove classes, your function should return a string containing the names of all of the classes you would like to remove.

The .hasClass() method returns true if any element in the matched set has the passed class. It returns false if none of them have the passed class. Keep in mind that if you pass it a matched set that has 100 <div> and only one of them has the passed class name, the method returns true:

```
// does any of the divs have the .bosco class?
var hasBosco = $("body > .container > .row > .col-md-4").
hasClass("bosco");
console.log("has bosco: " + hasBosco);
```

The `.toggleClass()` method is a time-saving convenience feature. Often, we will find ourselves simply adding a class if it doesn't exist and removing it if it does. This is exactly the scenario that `.toggleClass()` was created to solve. You pass it one or more classes to toggle on or off.

You can also pass `.toggleClass()` a second parameter, a boolean to indicate whether the class should be added or removed:

```
// remove the info class
var shouldKeepClass = false;
$("body > .container > .row > .col-md-4 .btn").toggleClass("btn-info",
shouldKeepClass);
```

The advantage this has over simply calling `.removeClass()` is that you can pass in the boolean as a variable and decide whether you want to add or remove the class at runtime.

Like its siblings, you can also pass a function to `.toggleClass()`. The function is passed an index that is the object's position in the matched set, the current class names, and the current state. It returns true to add the class and false to remove it.

Behavior classes

Normally, you add a class to an element in order to affect its appearance. Sometimes, you may want to add a class in order to affect how JavaScript processes the element. Why would you want to use a class for a behavior? This is because classes are booleans, and an element either has a given class or it doesn't. Properties, on the other hand, are key-value pairs, and you need to know whether property exists and what value it holds. This generally makes dealing with classes easier and, in some cases, syntactically cleaner than dealing with the equivalent property.

Attributes and properties

Before we get to the methods that deal with attributes and properties, we must first discuss a bigger issue: what's the difference between an attribute and a property? They are different, but how?

When the DOM is constructed from the HTML attributes, the key-value pairs that are included in the markup are built. Most of these attributes are translated into properties, which are placed onto the DOM element node. The important thing to understand is that once the element node is constructed, properties are used to keep track of the state of the node, not the attributes. Attributes are not updated as jQuery; if they are, JavaScript changes the DOM. They represent the state of the DOM when it was first loaded, and this is the problem. Think about a checkbox:

```
<input id="myCheckbox" type="checkbox" checked="checked" />
```

When the DOM parses this checkbox, it creates a checked property on the node for this element. It also creates a `defaultChecked` property in accordance with the rules laid out in the W3C specification. The difference between attributes and properties becomes clear. No matter how many times the user clicks on the checkbox, `.attr()` will always return `checked` because that was its state when the HTML was parsed. On the other hand, `.prop()` will alternate from "true" to "false" depending on the current actual state.

The `.attr()` method has been in jQuery since the beginning. It was originally used to both read and set the values of attributes and properties. This was a mistake; attributes and properties are different, but understanding the difference is difficult. In jQuery 1.6, the `.prop()` method was introduced and the scope of the `.attr()` method was limited to just attributes. This broke a lot of websites that had been using the `.attr()` method to set properties. This caused quite a furor among the jQuery community, which has since subsided. In general, if you want the current value of a property, use `.prop()` and not `.attr()`. Now that we understand the difference between attributes and properties, let's learn how to use the methods.

The `.attr()` method acts as both a getter and a setter of attributes. When used in the getter form, it will get the attribute of the first element in the matched set. It accepts only one parameter: the name of the attribute to be retrieved. When used in the setter form, it will set one or more attributes on all of the members of the matched set. You can call it in a few different ways. The first is with an attribute name in a string and its set value. The second is by passing it an object containing all of the attribute value pairs you wish to set. The final is with an attribute name and a function. The function will be passed an index and the old value of the attribute. It returns the desired set value. Here are some examples:

```
// setting an element attribute with an attribute and value
$("body > .container > .row > .col-md-4 .btn").attr("disabled",
"disabled");
// setting an element attribute with an object
```

```
$("body > .container > .row > .col-md-4 .btn").attr({"disabled":
"disabled"});
// setting an element attribute with a function
$("body > .container > .row > .col-md-4 .btn").attr("name",
function(index, attribute){
    return attribute + "_" + index;
});
```

The .prop() method is called in both its getter and setter forms in the same way as the .attr() method. In general, when manipulating properties of an element, this is the preferred method.

Keeping images proportional

Using the .attr() method, you can adjust the size of images by tweaking the height and width attributes. If you wish to keep the image size proportional without having to calculate the correct height for the width or vice versa, there is an easy cheat. Rather than changing both the width and height, remove the height attribute and only modify the width. The browser will then automatically adjust the height to proportionally match the width.

Removing attributes and properties

In order to remove an attribute from an element, we use .removeAttr(). You call it with either a single attribute name or with the names of several attributes separated by spaces. It has the extra benefit of not leaking memory when removing the attribute.

The .removeProp() method closely mirrors .removeAttr(). Keep in mind that you should only remove custom properties from an element, not native ones. If you remove native properties, such as checked, disabled, and so on, it can't be added back to the element. Instead of removing the property, you may want to set it to false using the .prop() method.

The .val() method is mainly used to retrieve values from form elements. It gets the value of the first element in a matched set from the input, select, and textarea method elements:

```
// retrieving data from an input tag with .val()
var firstName = $('#firstName').val();
console.log("First name:" + firstName);
var lastName = $('#lastName').val();
console.log("Last name:" + lastName);
```

It is easy to retrieve values from an input tag, as shown in the preceding code. The .val() method extracts the current string value of the element.

The type of data that's returned varies depending on the type of element it retrieves the data from. If it gets data from an input tag, the return type is a string. If the tag is selected with multiple attributes, then the return type is null if no items are selected. If one or more items are selected, then the return type is an array of strings, and each item in the array is the value of a selected option:

```
// .val() reading the value of a multiple select
var options = $('#vehicleOptions').val();
$.each(options, function (index, value) {
    console.log("item #" + index + " = " + value);
});
```

When used in its setter form, you can pass either a single string value, an array of strings, or a function to .val(). Passing a single string is the most typical use case. It does exactly what you'd expect: it sets the element's value:

```
// using .val() to set the last name field
$('#lastName').val("Robert");
```

When you pass in an array of strings to a select element with the multiple attribute set, it first clears any previously selected options, and then it selects all of the options whose values match those in the passed array:

```
// using .val() to select multiple new options
$('#vehicleOptions').val(["powerSeats", "moonRoof"]);
```

Like the other two methods, .attr() and .prop(), you can also pass in a function. jQuery will send two parameters to the function: an integer representing the elements index in the matched set and a value representing the element's current value. Your function should return a string that represents the element's new value.

To retrieve the HTML contents of an element, we use the .html() method. It returns the markup as a string:

```
// .html() getting some markup
var html = $('#testClass').html();
console.log("HTML: " + html);
```

When .html() is passed a string, it sets all of the elements of the matched set to the new markup. You can also pass a function to .html(). The function is passed to these parameters: an index and a string to hold the old HTML. You return a string from the function that holds the new HTML:

```
// .html() setting markup
$('#testClass').html("<div><h2>Hello there</h2></div>");
```

The `.text()` method retrieves the text content of all of the elements in the matched set. It is important to note that this method operates very differently from other methods in this regard. Normally, getters only get the data from the first element in the set. This method will concatenate the text from all of the elements, which can be a surprising result if you weren't expecting it:

```
// .text() getting text values
var comboText = $("select").text();
console.log(comboText);
```

It is important to note that the `.text()` method is for text, not HTML. If you try to send the HTML markup to it, it will not be rendered. As an example, let's try to send the same markup that we sent successfully to the `.html()` method:

```
// .text() trying to send HTML
$('#testClass').text("<div><h2>Hello there</h2></div>");
```

If we would like to add more HTML instead of replacing it, we can use the `.append()` and `.appendTo()` methods. They will both add the passed content to the end of the each element in the matched set. The difference between the two is readability, not functionality. With `.append()`, the selector comes first; then comes the new content. The `.appendTo()` method reverses this so that the new content comes before the selector:

```
// .append()
$("body > .container > .row > .col-md-4").append("<div><h2>Hello</
h2></div>");
// .appendTo()
$("<div><h2>Goodbye</h2></div>").appendTo("body > .container > .row >
.col-md-4");
```

The `.prepend()` and `.prependTo()` methods are just like `.append()` and `.appendTo()`, except that the content is placed at the beginning of each element instead of at the end:

```
// .prepend()
$("body > .container > .row > .col-md-4").prepend("<div><h2>Hello</
h2></div>");
// .prependTo()
$("<div><h2>Goodbye</h2></div>").prependTo("body > .container > .row >
.col-md-4");
```

The previous methods make the new content a child of the parent. The next few methods make the new content a sibling of the parent. The .after() and .insertAfter() methods add the new content as the sibling after the parent. Like .append() and .appendTo(), the only difference between the two is the order of the content and the selector:

```
// .after()
$("select").after("<h2>Hello</h2>");
// .insertAfter()
$("<h2>Goodbye</h2>").insertAfter("select");
```

The .before() and .insertBefore() methods add the new content as the sibling before the parent element. Again, the only difference between them is the order of the content and the selector:

```
// .before()
$("select").before("<h2>Hello</h2>");
// .insertBefore()
$("<h2>Goodbye</h2>").insertBefore("select");
```

The .wrap() method allows you to surround each member of a matched set with a new element:

```
// .wrap() surrounds the button with a border
$("a").wrap("<div style='border: 3px dotted black;'></div>");
```

This method should not be confused with the .wrapInner() method. The difference between the two is that .wrap() takes each member of the matched set and wraps it with a new element. However, .wrapInner() takes each of the children of the matched set and wraps them with the new content. The difference between these two methods is extremely clear in the example code. The .wrap() method surrounds each of the buttons, <a> tags with role=button, with a dotted border. The .wrapInner() method on the other hand, surrounds the text of the buttons with dotted borders:

```
// wrapInner() surrounds the button's text with a border
$("a").wrapInner("<div style='border: 3px dotted black;'></div>");
```

The .wrapAll() method surrounds all of the elements in the matched set with a new HTML element. Be careful with this method; it can radically change your web page. If the members of the set are widely separated, it can have a big and perhaps adverse effect. You definitely want to have the narrowest possible selector when using this method:

```
// wrapAll() everything
$("select").wrapAll("<div style='border: 3px dotted black;'></div>");
```

The last member of this group of methods is .unwrap(). It removes the parents of a matched set. Essentially, it is the inverse of .wrap():

```
// .unwrap() removes the divs we added earlier
$("a").unwrap();
```

Keeping with the theme of removing the markup, we have these methods: .remove(), .empty(), and .detach(). The first of these methods, .remove(), deletes the matched set of elements from the DOM. The elements and all of their children are removed:

```
// .remove() deletes the a tags from the page
$("a").remove();
```

The very closely related .empty() method also removes content from the DOM. The difference between the two is that .empty() deletes the children of the matched set, while .remove() deletes the matched elements themselves:

```
// .empty() keeps the a tags but deletes their text
$("a").empty();
```

The final method of the group, .detached(), behaves like the .remove() method with one difference: the removed content is returned to the caller as a set of jQuery objects. If you ever need to move the markup from one part of the web page to another, this is your method. Don't forget that you can use chaining on this method:

```
// .detach() deletes the a tags from the page and returns them to the
caller
var myButtons = $("a").detach();
$('hr:last').append(myButtons);
```

The .replaceAll() and the closely related .replaceWith() methods each replace the matched set with the passed content. The only difference between the two is the order of the selector and the content. In the .replaceWith() method, the selector comes first; then comes the new content. In the .replaceAll() method, the new content comes first:

```
// .replaceWith() replacing the selects with divs
$('select').replaceWith("<div>Replaced</div>");
```

The .clone() method makes a copy of the matched set of elements. It copies each element, and all of their children then return them to the caller as a jQuery object:

```
// .clone() makes a copy of the form then we insert the copy
$('.myForm').clone().insertBefore('.myForm');
```

Summary

This chapter has been a pretty arduous journey, but hopefully, you've seen that jQuery's DOM manipulation methods are logically thought out. We learned how to add content to the page before and after the existing elements. We also learned how to remove content from the page and even how to move content from one location to another.

We also learned that many jQuery methods have two different forms in order to provide us with a way to get the page content with one method and set it with another. There were also a couple of simple but handy bits of information on keeping our images proportional using the JSON object and determining the size of elements.

Even though we've learned a lot, our site is still static; after it executes its JavaScript, it doesn't do anything else. In the next chapter, we will change that. We will learn how to use events to allow our site to be interactive.

4
Events

In the previous chapters, we looked at how to find elements in the DOM and how to manipulate them after they are found. In this chapter, we actually start looking at how to build applications with jQuery and the important role that events play. Web applications use an event-driven programming model, so it is very important to understand events well. Without them, web apps — as we now know them — would not be possible. But before we go any further, let's look at what an event is.

An **event** is the occurrence of anything the system considers significant. It can originate in the browser, the form, the keyboard, or any other subsystem, and it can also be generated by the application via a trigger. An event can be as simple as a key press or as complex as the completion of an Ajax request.

While there are a myriad of potential events, events only matter when the application listens for them. This is also known as hooking an event. By hooking an event, you tell the browser that this occurrence is important to you and to let you know when it happens. When the event occurs, the browser calls your event handling code passing the event object to it. The event object holds important event data, including which page element triggered it. We will look at the event object in greater detail later in the chapter. Here is a list of the things we will cover in this chapter:

- The ready event
- Hooking and unhooking events
- Namespacing
- The event handler and object
- Passing data to an event
- Event shorthand methods
- Custom events
- Triggering events

The ready event

The first thing event programmers new to jQuery usually learn is the ready event, sometimes referred to as the **document ready event**. This event signifies that the DOM is fully loaded and that jQuery is open for business. The ready event is similar to the document load event except that it doesn't wait for all of the page's images and other assets to load. It only waits for the DOM to be ready. Also, if the ready event fires before it is hooked, the handler code will be called at least once, unlike most events. The .ready() event can only be attached to the document element. When you think about it, this makes sense since it fires when the DOM, is fully loaded.

The .ready() event has a few different hooking styles. All of the styles do the same thing: they hook the event. Which hook you use is up to you. In its most basic form, the hooking code looks like the following:

```
$(document).ready(handler);
```

Since it can only be attached to the document element, the selector can be omitted. In such a case, the event hook looks like this:

```
$().ready(handler);
```

The jQuery documentation does not recommend using the preceding form, however. There is a terser version of this event's hook. This version omits nearly everything and only passes an event handler to the jQuery function. It looks like this:

```
$(handler);
```

While all of the different styles work, I only recommend the first form since it is the most clear. While the other forms work and save a few bytes worth of characters, they do that at the expense of code clarity. If you are worried about the number of bytes an expression uses, you should use a JavaScript minimizer instead; it will do a much more thorough job of shrinking the code than you can ever do by hand.

The ready event can be hooked as many times as you'd like. When the event is triggered, the handlers are called in the order in which they were hooked. Let's take a look at an example via code:

```
// ready event style no# 1
    $(document).ready(function () {
        console.log("document ready event handler style no# 1");
    // we're in the event handler so the event has already fired.
    // let's hook it again and see what happens
        $(document).ready(function () {
        console.log("We get this handler even though the ready event
has already fired");
```

```
        });
        });
// ready event style no# 2
        $().ready(function () {
            console.log("document ready event handler style no# 2");
        });
// ready event style no# 3
        $(function () {
            console.log("document ready event handler style no# 3");
        });
```

In the preceding code, we hook the ready event three times, using a different hooking style each time. The handlers are called in the same order in which they are hooked. In the first event handler, we hook the event again. Since the event has been triggered already, we might expect that the handler will never be called, but we would be wrong. jQuery treats the ready event differently than other events. Its handler is always called, even if the event has already been triggered. This makes the ready event a great place for initialization and other code that must be run.

Hooking events

The ready event is different than all of the other events. Its handler will be called once, unlike the other events. It is also hooked differently than the other events. All of the other events are hooked by chaining the .on() method to the set of elements with which you wish to trigger the event. The first parameter passed to the hook is the name of the event, followed by the handling function, which can either be an anonymous function or the name of a function. This is the basic pattern for event hooking. It looks like this:

```
$(selector).on('event name', handling function);
```

The .on() method and its companion, the .off() method, were first added in version 1.7 of jQuery. For older versions of jQuery, the method used to hook the event is .bind(). Neither the .bind() method nor its companion, the .unbind() method, are deprecated, but .on() and .off() are preferred over them. If you are switching from .bind(), the call to .on() is identical at its simplest levels. The .on() method has capabilities beyond that of the .bind() method, which requires different sets of parameter to be passed to it. We will explore these capabilities later in this chapter.

If you would like more than one event to share the same handler, simply place the name of the next event after the previous with a space separating them:

```
$("#clickA").on("mouseenter mouseleave", eventHandler);
```

Unhooking events

The main method used to unhook an event handler is .off(), and calling it is simple. It looks like this:

```
$(elements).off('event name', handling function);
```

The handling function is optional, and the event name is optional as well. If the event name is omitted, then all events attached to the elements are removed. If the event name is included, then all handlers for the specified event are removed. This can create problems. Think about this scenario: you write a click event handler for a button. A bit later in the app's life cycle, someone else needs to know when the button is clicked on. Not wanting to interfere with already working code, they add a second handler. When their code is complete, they remove the handler, as follows:

```
$('#myButton').off('click');
```

Since the handler was called using only the event name, it removed not only the handler it added, but also all of the handlers for the click event. This is not what was wanted. Don't despair, however; there are two fixes for this problem:

```
function clickBHandler(event){
    console.log('Button B has been clicked, external');
}
$('#clickB').on('click', clickBHandler);
$('#clickB').on('click', function(event){
    console.log('Button B has been clicked, anonymous');
    // turn off the 1st handler without during off the 2nd
    $('#clickB').off('click', clickBHandler);
});
```

The first fix is to pass the event handler to the .off() method. In the preceding code, we placed two click event handlers on the button named clickB. The first event handler is installed using a function declaration, and the second is installed using an anonymous function. When the button is clicked on, both of the event handlers are called. The second one turns off the first by calling the .off() method and passing its event handler as a parameter. By passing the event handler, the .off() method is able to match the signature of the handler you'd like to turn off. If you are not using anonymous functions, this fix works well. But what if you want to pass an anonymous function as the event handler? Is there a way to turn off one handler without turning off the other? Yes, there is; the second fix is to use event namespacing.

Namespacing events

At times, it is necessary to be able to distinguish between different handlers for the same event without using the handler function. When this need arises, jQuery provides the ability to namespace events. To namespace an event, you add a period and the namespace to the name of the event. For example, to give the click event the namespace of `alpha`, perform this:

```
$("button").on("click.alpha", handler);
```

jQuery only allows you to create namespaces that are one level deep. If you add a second namespace, you don't create a second level; instead, you create a second namespace for the same event. Take a look at the following code:

```
$("button").on("click.alpha.beta", handler);
```

The preceding code is equivalent to creating two separate namespaces, such as the following:

```
$("button").on("click.alpha", handler);
$("button").on("click.beta", handler);
```

Using namespaces makes it possible for us to be more granular with our events, in the way we trigger them off and how we trigger them manually. We will explore how to trigger events programmatically later in this chapter.

The event handler

So far, we've just sort of glossed over the event handler. We've used it but not really explained it. It is time for us to correct that and look thoroughly at the event handler. Let's begin with what jQuery passes to the event handler. jQuery passes two things to every event handler: the `event` object and the `this` object. The `this` object is passed implicitly, which means that it is not a parameter like the `event` object. It is set by jQuery to point to the element to which the event handler is bound. The `this` object in JavaScript is somewhat like `this` in Java and C# or `self` in Objective-C; it points to the active object. This can be very handy, especially when a set of elements shares the same handler. The use of the `this` object makes it easy to act upon the correct element among many others:

```
$(document).ready(function(){
    // place a click event on the <li> tags
    $('ul> li').on('click', function(){
        console.log(this.id + " was clicked");
    });
});
```

In the preceding code, we place a click event on each of the `<li>` tags. We use the `this` object, which is implicitly passed to us, to tell which one of the `<li>` tags triggered the event. Also, note that we didn't use the event parameter since it was not needed for our example.

The event object

The event object, which is based on W3C specifications and is explicitly passed as a parameter to all event handlers, holds quite a few important properties, many of which may be useful to the event handler function. Because each event is different, so to be the values in the properties passed in the event object. Not every event populates every property, so some properties may be undefined. But there are a few properties that are universal, and we will explore them in detail next.

event.target

This is the element that triggered the event. This is not the same thing as the element bound to the event handler (the one pointed to by the `this` object). For example, if you click an `<a>` tag, which doesn't have a handler, but its parent, `<div>`, does, the event bubbles up to the parent. Under these conditions, `event.target` points to the `<a>` tag, but the `this` object points to the `<div>` element. Let's explore this with code:

```
$('#theParent').on('click', function (event) {
    console.log("this points to: "+this.id+", event.target points
    to: "+event.target.id);
    return false;
});
```

In the sample, we place a click event handler on the `<div>` tag that surrounds an `<a>` tag. There is no handler placed in `<a>`. When `<a>` is clicked on, since it doesn't have an elevator, it bubbles the event up to its parent, the `<div>` tag. The `this` object will now point to the `<div>` element, while `event.target` will still point to the `<a>` tag.

event.relatedTarget

The `relatedTarget` property also points to an element when valid, but rather than being the element that triggered the event, it is an element that is somehow related to the event instead. An easy way to see this is with the `mouseenter` event. Check out the following code:

```
$("form").on('mouseenter', function (event) {
    console.log("target is: " + event.target);
    console.log("relatedTarget is: " + event.relatedTarget);
});
```

When the `mouseenter` event is triggered, the `relatedTarget` property points to the element that will receive the `mouseleave` event. In our example, if we start on top `<a>` and move the cursor up and over the `<input>` tag, the related target will be the `<div>` tag that surrounds the `<a>` tag.

event.type

This property holds the name of the current event. It could come in handy if you use a single event handler for multiple events:

```
function eventHandler(event) {
    console.log("event type = " + event.type);
}
$("#clickA").on("mouseenter", eventHandler);
$("#clickB").on("mouseleave", eventHandler);
```

In the preceding code, we have two different events sharing the same handler. When either occurs, it displays the event type to enable us to tell them apart.

event.which

When a mouse or keyboard event occurs, this property can be used to tell which button or key was pressed. Let's take a quick look at a code sample:

```
$("#itemName").on('keypress', function (event) {
    console.log("key type: " + event.which);
});
```

When a key is pressed, the `which` property holds the key's code, which is a numeric value.

event.metaKey

This is a simple property, which holds a boolean value. It is set to `true` if the `metaKey` was pressed when the event fired or `false` if it was not. The `metaKey` method on the Macintosh keyboards is usually the command key; on Windows machines, it is the usually the Windows key.

event.pageX and event.pageY

The `pageX` and `pageY` properties hold the mouse position relative to the upper-left corner of the page. This could be useful when creating dynamic applications that update the page as the user moves the mouse like how it's done in a drawing program:

```
$(document).on('mousemove', function (event) {
    console.log("x position: " + event.pageX + ", y position: " +
    event.pageY);
});
```

In the code sample, we hook the `mousemove` event and display the current x and y position of the mouse dynamically.

event.originalEvent

When an event occurs, jQuery normalizes it so that the events in every browser behave in the same manner. Occasionally, jQuery's normalized event object lacks something that the original event object had and your application needs. jQuery places a complete copy of the original event object in the `originalEvent` property exactly for this reason.

Passing data to an event

If you ever need to pass data to an event, all you need to do is pass the data after the event name when hooking the event. You can pass nearly any type of data with a few caveats. First, if the data is a string, then you must also set the optional selector parameter that precedes it in the parameter list. If you don't need the selector parameter, you can set it to null. Second, the data that you pass can't be null or undefined. Here is a little sample that shows how to pass data to an event:

```
// here we pass an object
// we don't have to pass the selector param
$('#clickA').on('click',{msg: "The answer is: ", val: 42}, function
(event) {
    alert(event.data.msg + event.data.val);
    return false;
});
// here we pass a string as the data param.
// Note the null selector param
$('clickB').on('click', null, "The answer is 42.", function(event){
    alert(event.data);
    return false;
});
```

In the second event hook, we pass a null selector parameter in order to avoid confusion since we are passing a string as the data parameter.

Event shorthand methods

Web programming is event-driven, and some events are used so often that jQuery has created shorthand methods to hook them. The following two methods are equal:

```
$(element).on('click', handling function);
$(element).click(handling function);
```

The second form is shorter and possibly easier to read, but there is a downside. In the shorthand form, there is no way to add the extra and optional parameters. If you need the selector or data parameters, then you must use the longhand form. Here is a list of all of the shorthand methods:

```
.change();
.click();
.dblclick();
.error();
.focus();
.focusin();
.focusout();
.hover();
.keydown();
.keypress();
.keyup();
.load();
.mousedown();
.mouseenter();
.mouseleave();
.mousemove();
.mouseout();
.mouseover();
.resize();
.scroll();
.select();
.submit();
```

Creating your own events

Creating your own events is common practice in JavaScript. There are a lot of reasons for this. For one, it is a best practice since it promotes the loose coupling of code. Code that uses events to communicate isn't tightly coupled. This is easy to do; you create event handlers for your own events in the same way that you create handlers for system events. Imagine that we need to create an event and would like to call `superDuperEvent`. Here is the code that creates its handler:

```
$(document).on('superDuperEvent', function (event) {
    console.log(event.type + " triggered");
});
$('#clickA').click(function(){
    $(document).trigger('superDuperEvent');
})
```

In the code, we create two event handlers. The first creates a handler for our `superDuperEvent method`. If the code looks nearly identical to the handler code we've created for system events, then that is the way it is intended.

Triggering events

Once you have created the handler code for your custom event, the next question you need to answer is this: how do you trigger the event? This is something we haven't mentioned yet, but all you need is the `.trigger()` method. The `.trigger()` method executes all of the handlers bound to the matched set of elements for the event type. As the preceding code shows, all we need to do in order to trigger our custom event is call the `.trigger()` method on the set of elements and pass in the event's name.

If we'd like, we can also pass custom data to the event's handler. And again, this is the same as what we've done with regular events. We simply call the `.trigger()` method, and after we pass the event name, we pass the custom data:

```
$(document).on('superDuperEvent', function (event, message) {
    console.log(event.type + " triggered with message: " +
    message);
});
$('#clickA').click(function(){
    $(document).trigger('superDuperEvent', ["Hello from the
    trigger function at: "+(new Date()).getTime()]);
})
```

As the preceding code shows, passing data to our event's handler can do one thing that passing data bound to the event hook can't: we can pass fresh data. When we pass data in the event hook, it never changes, which limits its usefulness. But the data in the trigger can be changed each time we call the event. Take a look at this code sample:

```
$(document).on('superDuperEvent', function (event, message) {
    console.log(event.type + " triggered with message: " +
    message);
});
$('#clickA').click(function(){
    $(document).trigger('superDuperEvent', ["Hello from the
    trigger function at: "+(new Date()).getTime()]);
});
```

Each time our custom event is triggered, we pass it the current time in milliseconds. Passing fresh data is not possible when hooking events.

The death of the .live() and .die() methods

As of version 1.7 of jQuery, both the .live() method and its companion, the .die() method, have been deprecated. And they were both removed from the library as of version 1.9. While they still exist within the jQuery Migrate Plugin, they should not be used to write new code, and any old code using them should be rewritten. A lot of users really liked these methods, especially the .live() method. It was used to write very dynamic code. So, why were these methods removed from the library?

The jQuery documentation does a great job of listing some of the problems with the .live() method. First among them was its performance. The .live() method, in spite of what was passed in the selector, was actually bound to the document element. Yet, it would still retrieve the set of elements specified by the selector, which could be time consuming on large documents. When an event occurred, it had to bubble all the way up to the document before it could be handled. This meant that every event handled by .live() was guaranteed to take the longest, slowest path to its handler function.

The .live() method didn't behave similar to other jQuery methods, and this led to bugs. It didn't support chaining events, though it looked like it did. Calling event. stopProgation() does nothing since there is nothing at a level higher than the document. It also didn't play well with other events. So, it was decided to deprecate this event and remove it eventually.

Looking deeper at .on()

The `.on()` method is not just a renamed `.bind()` method. It has capabilities that the former lacked. Part of the reason for these new capabilities is to give developers a way to write code in a fashion similar to what the `.live()` method provided.

The `.on()` method has an optional parameter; the which selector is a string. Most of the time, it isn't required, so either it isn't passed, or a null is passed instead. When you'd like to replace the `.live()` method without its inefficiencies, use the `.on()` method:

```
$(document).ready(function (event) {
    var count = 0;
        // hooks the live replacement
    $('#holder').on('click', "li", function (event) {
        console.log("<li> clicked: " + this.id);
    });
    // clicking on the a button will add another element to the ul
    $('#clickA').on('click', function (event) {
        var id = "Li_" + count++;
        $('#holder').append('<li id="' + id + '">' + id +
        '</li>');
    });
});
```

In the preceding code, we hook two events. We first hook the parent element, the `<ul>` tag, which will serve as a container for all of the `<li>` tags: those that exist now and those that will be created later. Then, we hook the button that will be used to generate new `<li>` tags. Each time we create a new tag, we increment a counter and concatenate it to the string used for the new tags id and then append it to the `<ul>` tag.

Summary

We've learned a lot about one of the most important things in web programming: events. Events make websites interactive. We began by looking at one of the most important events, the jQuery ready event. We continued to cover hooking and unhooking events, namespacing, and finally, writing event handlers using the event object. With the basics covered, we showed how to write your own events and trigger them.

In the next chapter, we will learn how to make our site smooth and polished using jQuery's built-in and custom animations. Animations help ease the transition from one application state to the next. Without it, a site can seem jarring to a user when elements on the page appear and disappear abruptly.

5
Making Your Site Snazzy with jQuery

It is easy to underestimate the importance animation has for any modern, polished web application. At times, it can seem frivolous and nearly gratuitous to waste time adding animations since they don't seem to add anything to the application. But for users, animations make a huge difference. They help ease the transition from one application state to the next. They also help give the user a sense of location. When a user clicks on a button that causes the page to shift to the left and clicking another button causes the page to shift back to the right, the user derives a sense of location from the animation. In this chapter, we will learn how use jQuery animation and effects to make our site snazzy.

We will cover the following topics:

- The importance of animation
- Hiding and showing elements
- Sliding elements around
- Creating custom effects
- Using effects correctly

The importance of animations

As developers, it is easy for us to forget how abstract our applications can be. The concept of a *home* is embedded in our developer brains, but there is nothing really homey about one page of our site compared to any another. But if all of the other pages appear to center on one page without even labeling it, that becomes the home page in the eyes of most users.

Animation effects help when transitioning from one application state to the next. Without animation, it is easy to miss when elements are added to or removed from the page. The trick is to be skilled in the use of animation. Animations should never feel like they are impeding the user from their goals.

Hiding and showing elements

Let's take a look at animations in jQuery with two of the most useful ones: `hide` and `show`. jQuery provides us with the `.hide()` and `.show()` methods, which do exactly what their names suggest. Straight out of the box, these two methods don't animate; they act as simple switches, immediately hiding or showing the attached set of elements. However, both of them have several ways it can be called. First, let's take a look at the `.hide()` method, and then look at its companion, the `.show()` method.

In its most basic mode, the `.hide()` method is called with no parameters, as follows:

```
$(elements).hide();
```

When called like this, it immediately hides the specified set of elements. Internally, jQuery adds a style attribute to the elements with the property of "display: none". This means that the element is both invisible and gives up its space in the DOM. The `.hide()` method accepts optional parameters as well:

```
$(elements).hide(duration, easing, complete);
```

The first parameter is duration. It can be either a string or an integer. If it is an integer, it is the number of milliseconds the complete animation should take. If it is a string, it must be one of the two supplied convenience names for duration, either `fast` or `slow`. Fast is equivalent to 200 milliseconds and slow is equivalent to 600 milliseconds.

In its basic mode, the `.show()` method is also called with no parameters, as follows:

```
$(elements).show();
```

When called like this, it will immediately show the specified set of elements. jQuery will remove the style attribute with the property of "display: none;". The `.show()` method accepts parameters identical to those of the `.hide()` method.

Let's take a more practical look at using these methods:

```
<body>
<div>
<button id="hide">Hide Pics</button>
<button id="show">Show Pics</button>
</div>
```

```
<div id="allPictures">
<img id="picture1" src="http://lorempixel.com/160/100/nature/1"
class="thumbnail"/>
<img id="picture2" src="http://lorempixel.com/160/100/nature/2"
class="thumbnail"/>
<img id="picture3" src="http://lorempixel.com/160/100/nature/3"
class="thumbnail"/>
<img id="picture4" src="http://lorempixel.com/160/100/nature/4"
class="thumbnail"/>
</div>
<script type="text/javascript">
    $(document).ready(function () {
        var $hide = $('#hide'),
            $show = $('#show'),
            $allPictures = $('#allPictures');

        $hide.click(function () {
            $allPictures.hide();
        });
        $show.click(function () {
            $allPictures.show();
        });
    });
</script>
```

In our example app, we have four thumbnail images supplied by the super useful site, lorem pixel (`http://lorempixel.com`). Lorem pixel supplies web designers with placeholder images, which are used while building your site. These images should not be used in production.

The placeholder URL consists of the host site, followed by the width and height of the desired image in pixels. The category of the image is next; in our case, it is `nature`, and the final number identifies a specific picture. There is detailed information on the lorem pixel site on how to create your own URL for placeholder images.

Above the images is a set of buttons that trigger actions on the thumbnails. The buttons are cached in the `$hide` and `$show` variables. When the hide button is clicked on, we hide the images. When the show button is clicked on, we do the opposite and show the images. Take note of the way we cache the jQuery objects by storing them in JavaScript objects rather than looking them up again. Caching them results in speed improvement when they are used again. In this small app, it makes no difference, but it can result in a significant increase in speed in more complex apps. We will discuss this in more detail in *Chapter 7, Talking to Your Server*.

In order to make it easier to know which variables hold jQuery objects, we have adopted the standard of beginning such variables with the dollar sign, $. Some developers don't like the use of mnemonic devices in variable names, but I find it helps a lot, especially when reading code written by other developers on my team.

`hide` and `show` are so closely related that jQuery has a special method that executes both. The `.toggle()` method will hide the elements when they are shown and show the elements when they are hidden. It is a more appropriate method for our use case, so let's modify the code:

```
$(document).ready(function () {
    var $hide = $('#hide'),
        $show = $('#show'),
        $toggle = $('#toggle'),
        $allPictures = $('#allPictures');

    $hide.click(function () {
        $allPictures.hide();
    });
    $show.click(function () {
        $allPictures.show();
    });
    $toggle.click(function () {
        $allPictures.toggle();
    });
});
```

We've only had to change a few lines of our code. First, we needed a variable to hold the toggle button. Then, we added code to hook the click of the toggle button, and finally, we made a call to the `.toggle()` method. A nice thing about the toggle button is that we can just continuously click on it and it will keep on toggling the state of the pictures.

Hiding and showing the pictures is interesting, but not exactly thrilling. So, let's add duration to the code. Here are the modifications to the app:

```
$(document).ready(function () {
    var $hide = $('#hide'),
        $show = $('#show'),
        $toggle = $('#toggle'),
        $allPictures = $('#allPictures');
```

```
$hide.click(function () {
    $allPictures.hide('slow');
});
$show.click(function () {
    $allPictures.show('fast');
});
$toggle.click(function () {
    $allPictures.toggle(1500);
});
});
```

This time, we've made changes to only three lines. Each of the lines calls one of the effect methods. We're passing `slow` to the `.hide()` method, `fast` to the `.show()` method, and `1500` to the `.toggle()` method. Remember, when an integer is passed to an effect method, it is the time in milliseconds, so 1,500 means 1.5 seconds.

Adding some duration to the effects we have so far is more appealing than simply turning the elements on and off, but it might be nice to have the images fade in and out instead of shrinking and growing. Luckily, jQuery has us covered with some methods that do exactly that: fade out and fade in.

.fadeOut()

The `.fadeOut()` method gradually reduces the CSS opacity property down to 0 so that the elements are no longer visible, and then it sets the display property to `none`. This method has parameters identical to `.hide()`.

.fadeIn()

The `.fadeIn()` method does the opposite of the `.fadeOut()` method. It first sets the display property to increase the opacity property to 1 so that the elements are fully opaque.

.fadeToggle()

Just like the `.toggle()` method, the `.fadeToggle()` method will fade out elements if they are visible and fade in elements if they are not visible.

For a more practical example, let's replace the `.hide()`, `.show()`, and `.toggle()` methods with `.fadeOut()`, `.fadeIn()`, and `.fadeToggle()`, respectively:

```
$(document).ready(function () {
    var $hide = $('#hide'),
        $show = $('#show'),
```

```
        $toggle = $('#toggle'),
        $allPictures = $('#allPictures');

    $hide.click(function () {
        $allPictures.fadeOut('slow');
    });
    $show.click(function () {
        $allPictures.fadeIn('fast');
    });
    $toggle.click(function () {
        $allPictures.fadeToggle(1500);
    });
});
```

In the preceding code, we've replaced the hide/show methods with their fade equivalents. The code still functions as it did earlier, only now, we have a new animation effect: fading.

So far, we've only used the duration parameter, but we know that there are two more: `easing` and `complete`. Let's check out `complete` first because it is fairly easy to understand.

The complete parameter is a function that is called once the animation is finished. It is not passed any parameters explicitly, but it is implicitly passed the `this` object pointing to the animated element. We can see this in action by making a small modification to our example program:

```
$toggle.click(function () {
    $allPictures.fadeToggle(1500, function () {
        alert("Hola: "+this.id);
    });
});
```

After the duration, we add an inline anonymous function, which is called once the animation is complete. The `this` object points to the animated element, so we display its `id` in an alert message box. The complete function is called once for every animated element, which may be surprising. In our current example, we are animating the contents of a `<div>` that holds the images. Consider that we change our code to the following:

```
$toggle.click(function () {
    $('img').fadeToggle(1500, function () {
        alert("Hola: "+this.id);
    });
});
```

By changing our code to point to the individual <img> tags instead of their parent <div> container, the complete function is now called once for each of the tags, and we will see the alerts walk through the <img> tags one by one.

The easing parameter deals with how animating objects move. In the real world, objects rarely move at a constant speed. Think of a train leaving a station. It slowly builds up speed as it pulls away. It slowly accelerates until it reaches its desired speed, and then at some point, it will begin to slow down as it approaches the next station. If we were to graph the train's speed, it would be a curve, not a straight line. This acceleration and deceleration of objects seems natural to us since it is the way things move in nature, whether it is a train, a cheetah chasing a gazelle, or us as we get up from our desk to get a glass of water.

Out of the box, jQuery comes with two easings: the default one named swing and a second one called linear. We have been using swing in all of the examples so far since it is the default. Let's also take a look at linear and compare the two:

```
<div>
<button id="hide">Hide Pics</button>
<button id="show">Show Pics</button>
<button id="toggleSwing">Toggle Swing Pics</button>
<button id="toggleLinear">Toggle Linear Pics</button>
</div>
<div id="allPictures">
<img id="picture1" src="http://lorempixel.com/160/100/nature/1"
class="thumbnail"/>
<img id="picture2" src="http://lorempixel.com/160/100/nature/2"
class="thumbnail"/>
<img id="picture3" src="http://lorempixel.com/160/100/nature/3"
class="thumbnail"/>
<img id="picture4" src="http://lorempixel.com/160/100/nature/4"
class="thumbnail"/>
</div>
<script type="text/javascript">
    $(document).ready(function () {
        var $hide = $('#hide'),
            $show = $('#show'),
$toggleSwing = $('#toggleSwing'),
$toggleLinear = $('#toggleLinear'),
            $allPictures = $('#allPictures');

        $hide.click(function () {
            $allPictures.fadeOut('slow');
        });
        $show.click(function () {
```

```
            $allPictures.fadeIn('fast');
        });
    $toggleSwing.click(function () {
            $allPictures.fadeToggle(1500, "swing");
        });
        $toggleLinear.click(function () {
            $allPictures.fadeToggle(1500, "linear");
        });
    });
</script>
```

In the preceding code, we get rid of the toggle button and replace it with two new toggles: one using `"swing"` and the other using `"linear"`. We also create two event handlers to implement the appropriate fade in and fade out. While the difference between the two easings is subtle, it is there. It is more noticeable when objects are moving around. So, in the next section, we will introduce the slide animation and see how our two easings look with it.

Sliding elements around

The next sets of methods is called just like the previous two sets. The slide methods are very similar to the show and hide methods, except that instead of shrinking and growing the set elements' width and height dimensions, only the height is changed.

.slideUp()

The `.slideUp()` method shrinks the height of the set of elements down to zero, and then it sets the display property to `none`. The method takes the same three optional parameters that have been discussed already: `duration`, `easing`, and `complete`:

```
$(elements).slideUp([duration],[easing], [complete]);
```

.slideDown()

The `.slideDown()` method grows the height of the set of elements to 100%. Its call looks like this:

```
$(elements).slideDown([duration],[easing], [complete]);
```

.slideToggle()

The final member of this set is the `.slideToggle()` method, which will alternate the set of elements between the shown and hidden states:

```
$(elements).slideDown([duration],[easing], [complete]);
```

We've modified our code to use the slide methods instead of the fade methods. The easing methods are more noticeably different now. Here is the changed code:

```
$hide.click(function () {
    $allPictures.slideUp('slow');
});
$show.click(function () {
    $allPictures.slideDown('fast');
});
$toggleSwing.click(function () {
    $allPictures.slideToggle(1500, "swing");
});
$toggleLinear.click(function () {
    $allPictures.slideToggle(1500, "linear");
});
```

Since the jQuery animation methods are all called similarly, we were able to simply replace the words `fadeOut`, `fadeIn`, and `fadeToggle` with their slide equivalents.

I think we have spent enough time studying the basic animation effects. The real fun and graphical wow is in the custom effects.

Creating custom effects

jQuery doesn't include many effects; out of the box, there are just the hide and show, fade in and fade out, and slide methods. If these were all it could include, it would probably not have been worth including them in the library. Luckily, jQuery lets us create our own animations.

.animate()

Understanding the `.animate()` method is the key to understanding how to create custom effects. While the other methods are important, none of them do anything until you get the animate method working, which isn't too hard luckily, especially if you keep in mind how the animate property actually works. It works by manipulating the value of CSS properties. Most—but not all—properties can be manipulated. Let's take a quick look in order to better explain how the `.animate()` method works:

```
<div>
<button id="hide">Hide Pics</button>
<button id="show">Show Pics</button>
<button id="toggleSwing">Animate Swing Pics</button>
<button id="toggleLinear">Animate Linear Pics</button>
```

```
</div>
<div id="allPictures" style="position: relative;">
<img id="picture1" src="http://lorempixel.com/160/100/nature/1"
class="thumbnail"/>
<img id="picture2" src="http://lorempixel.com/160/100/nature/2"
class="thumbnail"/>
<img id="picture3" src="http://lorempixel.com/160/100/nature/3"
class="thumbnail"/>
<img id="picture4" src="http://lorempixel.com/160/100/nature/4"
class="thumbnail"/>
</div>
<script type="text/javascript">
    $(document).ready(function () {
        var $hide = $('#hide'),
                $show = $('#show'),
                $toggleSwing = $('#toggleSwing'),
                $toggleLinear = $('#toggleLinear'),
                $allPictures = $('#allPictures');

        $hide.click(function () {
            $allPictures.slideUp('slow');
        });
        $show.click(function () {
            $allPictures.slideDown('fast');
        });
        $toggleSwing.click(function () {
    $allPictures.animate({left: "+=200"}, 1500, "swing");
        });
        $toggleLinear.click(function () {
    $allPictures.animate({left: "-=200"}, 1500, "linear");
        });
```

We've made a few more modifications to our venerable example. We've changed the text of the buttons, added the two `.animate()` methods, and also had to add a style of position that's relative to `allPictures<div>`. The addition of the position relative is critical, and its absence can be the source of a great deal of animation frustration. jQuery's animate function doesn't change the rules of CSS. In order to move `<div>`, it must be moveable. Elements missing a position property default to being position static, which means that they are positioned with the layout of the page and can't be moved. So if you try to animate it, nothing will happen. Placing `<div>` in relative positioning means that it can be moved relative to its layout position.

The .animate() method takes the three parameters that we've already become familiar with—duration, easing, and complete—and adds a new one: properties, which include the one or more CSS properties we wish to animate. The value of the property can either be absolute or relative. If you simply put a value in the property, it is absolute. jQuery will animate to the value. If you attempt to run an absolute animation a second time, nothing will happen since the property will already hold the desired value. Relative values, on the other hand, are more directional. In the earlier example app, we use two different relative property values. The first one tells jQuery to animate <div> 200 pixels to the right. The second one, attached to the toggle linear button, tells jQuery to move <div> 200 pixels to the left. To use a relative value, just wrap the value in quotes and precede it with either +=xx or -=xx, where xx is the amount to change the property.

You can modify more than one property at a time. When you add more properties, jQuery will animate each to its value:

```
$toggleSwing.click(function () {
    $allPictures.animate({
        left: "+=200",
        top: "+=200",
        opacity: "-=1"
    }, 1500, "swing");
});
$toggleLinear.click(function () {
        $allPictures.animate({
        left: "-=200",
        top: "-=200",
        opacity: "+=1"
    }, 1500, "linear");
});
```

In the preceding example, we've added two more properties to each .animate() method: top and opacity, both of which are relative like the left property. An important thing to note about the animate method is that unlike the show/hide, fade, or slide methods, it never adds the "display: none" style to the element. Even when the opacity is 0, the element still occupies all of its space on the page.

.delay()

Animations can run sequentially one after the other by chaining the animate methods together. You can also introduce a delay in the animation using the .delay() method. It takes two parameters: duration and queue name. Duration tells you how long in milliseconds you should pause the animation engine for, and queueName is the name of the queue to be delayed. We won't use named queues in this book, so we won't talk about the queue name:

```
$toggleSwing.click(function () {
    $allPictures
            .animate({
                left: "+=200"
            }, 1500, "swing")
            .delay(1000)
            .animate({
                top: "+=200",
                opacity: "-=1"
            }, 1500, "swing");
});
$toggleLinear.click(function () {
    $allPictures
            .animate({
                top: "-=200",
                opacity: "+=1"
            }, 1500, "linear")
            .delay(1000)
            .animate({
                left: "-=200"
            }, 1500, "linear");
});
```

In this example, we chain together two separate animations with a 1 second delay between them. Note that if you rapidly press either button, pretty soon, <div> will disappear off the page and might not be visible again. This problem is caused by the fact that jQuery adds each new animation request to a queue. It is pretty easy to add items to the queue faster than jQuery can execute them. We will take a look at this problem in the next section.

r5

.queue(), .dequeue(), and .clearQueue()

The queue methods give us access to the animation queue that jQuery uses to run the animations. jQuery allows us to have more than one queue, but there is seldom a need for more than one. The `.queue()` method can be used to both get and set either the standard animation queue or a custom one. We can use the queue method to see how many items are in the current queue, and we can pass a callback function to it that is called once the queue is empty.

The `.dequeue()` method is handy when the queue has been stopped and a new item has been added to it. In order to get the queue going again, the `.dequeue()` method must be called. The `.clearQueue()` method removes all of the queued up items that haven't yet executed from the queue.

.stop() and .finish()

The `.stop()` method stops the current animation. If there are callbacks associated with an animation running, they are not called. The `.finish()` method is very similar to this, except that it does everything. It stops the running animation, clears the queues, and completes all the animations for the matched set.

jQuery.fx.interval and jQuery.fx.off

These are two global variables within jQuery. The `jQuery.fx.interval` method sets the animation rate. The lower the value, the faster and possibly smoother the animation. In general, you probably don't want to mess around with this value. It is the global animation timer. Changing it changes the timing for all the animations, not just yours. The `jQuery.fx.off` method kills all the animations when set to true.

Using effects correctly

When jQuery encounters a new bit of animation that it needs to do, it places the new animation at the end of the animation queue. While this is mostly a great way to handle things, it is possible that it might overwhelm the queue by putting items into it faster than they can be pulled out. In general, you should take care when adding more items into the queue. You may want to clear the queue before adding more items to it.

While the animation features of jQuery are very convenient, they are not exactly state of the art, and they are start showing their age. An example can be seen in the jQuery source code. The following code comes from the source code of jQuery version 2.1.1:

```
jQuery.fx.start = function() {
    if ( !timerId ) {
        timerId = setInterval( jQuery.fx.tick, jQuery.fx.interval
    );
    }
};
```

When running an animation, jQuery uses the `setInterval()` method to time each animation frame; in fact, the `jQuery.fx.interval` global value is used as the timer value. While this was cool a few years ago, most modern browser use the `window.requestAnimationFrame()` method instead, and for browsers that lack it, there are polyfills available. The end of effect of using the `setInterval` method instead of `requestAnimationFramework` is that jQuery's animation will always seem a bit flicker even in the latest browser on the fastest hardware since there is no coordination between the rendering of a frame and the `setInterval` method, like there is with `requestAnimationFrame`.

Summary

We covered a lot of code this chapter. Animations may seem to be easy to code, but when done well, they can add a lot of content to an application and help make the user aware of the application state change. We first learned how to use jQuery's easy-to-use, built-in animation methods. Once we understood them, we moved on to the `.animate()` and `.delay()` methods, which allow us to create our own custom animation.

We closed the chapter with a bit of information about the way jQuery performs animations. While it is fine in the simple examples shown, it is actually a bit antiquated. If you wish to perform more complicated animations, you might want to look at more sophisticated libraries, such as `Velocity.js`, `GSAP`, or others.

In the next chapter, we will look at submitting data via forms with jQuery. In particular, we will look at how to validate our forms before we send data to our server.

6
Better Forms with jQuery

In the last chapter, we looked at animations and how they can bring your site to life. In this chapter, we will look at one of the most important functions of any website – forms. A well-crafted form can be the difference between a new customer and a missed opportunity. So forms deserved to be examined closely.

Getting users to complete a form and submit it can be challenging. If our site frustrates a user at any time, they may abandon the form and our site. So we provide the user with gentle cues letting them know what each input element of the form needs by using tool tips, placeholder text, and visual indicators letting them know whether an input is valid or invalid.

jQuery doesn't have too many methods dealing specifically with forms. The first of them are all shortcut methods; they replace using `.on()` with the name of the event as the first parameter. Let's examine them and learn how to put them to use.

Employing form methods

Let's have a look at a number of jQuery methods used with forms.

.submit()

The most important of the form methods is `.submit()`. It binds a handler to the browser submit event. When the user has, hopefully, filled out your form and clicks the submit button, the event handler here gets activated. If you want to handle this event yourself without the form actually being submitted, you must either call `event.preventDefault()` or return `false` from the method. If you don't do one of these things, the form will be submitted to your server.

```
// Cancel the default action by returning false from event handler
$('form').submit(function(event){
    alert('submit');
    return false;
});
```

In the preceding event handler, we return `false` to keep the browser from submitting our form. We could have also called `event.preventDefault()`. We could have written the preceding as:

```
// Cancel the default action by call
$('form').on('submit', function(event){
    alert('submit');
    event.preventDefault();
});
```

This example works identically to the first, but uses a bit more text. We replaced the submit shortcut method with its long form, the `.on()` method, and we also replaced the return false by directly calling the `preventDefault()` method of the event object.

.focus()

When the user either tabs or clicks on a form element, the browser fires a focus event. The focus method creates a handler for this event. This could be handy if you would like to create some kind of indication for your users that this is the active element. Check out the `.blur()` method's code example to see how to use it with `.focus()`.

It is important to note that only form elements can receive focus. All of the following are form elements:

- `<input>`
- `<select>`
- `<textarea>`
- `<button>`

.blur()

The `.blur()` method is the companion to the `.focus()` method. It creates a handler that is triggered when the user tabs off of or otherwise leaves this element causing it to lose focus. This event could also be used to run a validation of the element, but the change event is actually a better choice and it will be explained shortly with the `.change()` method.

```
// Adds / removes the active class using the focus/blur events
$("input, textarea").focus(function(event){
    $(this).addClass('active');
});

$("input, textarea").blur(function(event){
    $(this).removeClass('active');
});
```

We can use the `.focus()` and `.blur()` methods together to add a class to the active element and remove it once it loses focus to offer a better visual cue to our users. Note that we are hooking both the input elements and the text area element by separating the tag names with a comma.

One potential problem with the `.focus()` and `.blur()` methods is that they don't bubble up. If you place a child element that is to receive focus within a parent element and hook the focus event of the parent, the event will never be triggered. This means that you can't delegate these events to their parent. You will also have trouble if you need to hook the focus/blur events of dynamically generated input tags.

```
// These handlers will never be triggered
$('#fiOne').focus(function (event) {
    console.info('Focus: ' + this.id + ', triggered by: ' + event.
target.id);
    $(this).addClass('active');
});

$('#fiOne').blur(function (event) {
    console.info('Blur: ' + this.id + ', triggered by: ' + event.
target.id);
    $(this).removeClass('active');
});
```

In the preceding code we hook the focus and blur events of the fieldset, fiOne, which is the parent element for all of the radio buttons. There is no handler for those events on any of the radio button children. Unfortunately, since neither event bubbles up to its parent element, no event is ever triggered.

.focusin() and .focusout()

So now we know that neither the focus nor the blur events bubble up to their parent. We've also learned in previous chapters how bubbling can help us to create more dynamic applications. Is there any way that we can get around the lack of bubbling? Luckily, there is a solution: the .focusin() and .focusout() methods. The .focusin() method creates a handler for the focusin event, which is triggered when an element is about to receive focus. The .focusout() method is the same as the .focusin() method except it works with the focusout event, which is triggered when an element is about to lose focus. Both of these methods will bubble up to their parent element.

```
// These handlers use the focusin/focusout, which bubble up
$('#fiOne').focusin(function (event) {
    console.info('Focusin: ' + this.id + ', triggered by: ' + event.
target.id);
    $(this).addClass('active');
});

$('#fiOne').focusout(function (event) {
    console.info('Focusout: ' + this.id + ', triggered by: ' + event.
target.id);
    $(this).removeClass('active');
});
```

This code sample is nearly identical to the previous sample, except the focus and blur events have been replaced with the focusin and focusout events, respectively. We again hook the parent fieldset element. This time, however, the events bubble up to their parent. We add the active class to the fieldset and even display which element generated the event by getting its ID from the target property of the event object.

```
// Adds an input tag dynamically by clicking the "Add Another" button
var inputCounter = 0;
$('#addAnother').click(function (event) {
    console.info("Adding another");
    $('#inputMomma').append($("<input>").attr({'type': 'text',
    'id': 'newInput' + inputCounter++}));
});

// Makes the parent element the active class
$('#inputMomma').focusin(function (event) {
    console.info('Focusin: ' + this.id + ', triggered by: ' +
    event.target.id);
    $(this).addClass('active');
```

```
    });

    // Removes the active class from the parent
    $('#inputMomma').focusout(function (event) {
        console.info('FocusOut: ' + this.id + ', triggered by: ' +
        event.target.id);
        $(this).removeClass('active');
    });
```

In this example, we use jQuery to dynamically create new input tags. Please note how we use chaining to both append the new input tag and set its attributes. Even though these tags don't exist at the time their parent hooks the `focusin` and `focusout` events, they nonetheless bubble their events to it.

.change()

The `.change()` method creates a handler for the change event. What is nice about the change event is it fire only when the value of the input or text element has changed and the field no longer has focus. This makes it better for validation than using the blur event since the blur event always fires when the element loses focus, whether or not its value has changed. By using the change event, we save ourselves from doing some unnecessary processing.

```
    // only called once focus is lost and contents have changed
    $("input, textarea").change(function (event) {
        console.info('Change is good:' + this.id);
    });
```

.select()

The last of the event handler methods that we will examine in this chapter is the `.select()` method. It binds to the select event. This event is only triggered on the two elements that allow you to type in text: `<textarea>` and `<input type='text'>`. The select event only occurs when the user selects some text.

```
    // Triggered when some text is selected
    $('textarea').select(function(event){
        console.info("Something was selected: " + this.tagName);
    });
```

In this example, we simply hook the select event and display the name of the tag when it is received. Like most events, we can also trigger the select event by using the `.trigger()` method.

```
// Selects all of the textarea text
$('#selectText').click(function (event) {
    console.info("Adding another");
    $('textarea').select();
});
```

This snippet selects all of the text in the `textarea` and also gives `<textarea>` the focus. Other shortcomings of the select event are that there is no standard way to retrieve the selected text or to declare the range of characters to select. When the select event is fired, it always selects all of the characters. There are jQuery plugins available to fill the gap.

Tooltips

The title attribute has been available since HTML 4.01 for all elements except `<base>`, `<basefont>`, `<head>`, `<html>`, `<meta>`, `<param>`, `<script>`, and `<title>`. It defines a string that most browsers will render above and near the element when the cursor is above the element. The displayed string is commonly referred to as a tooltip.

Standard HTML tooltips leave a lot to be desired. Out of the box they are usually styled in a very plain fashion that may clash with your site. If your site, for example, uses a large font to aid your users, a standard tooltip will look very awkward. Luckily, jQuery has a solution, although it is not in the core library.

jQuery UI is a library that contains a set of user interface components. The set is designed to be customizable. One of the members of the set is the tooltip. For browsers that lack a native tooltip (title attribute support), it adds support. For browsers that have native support for tooltips, it enhances them by make them customizable and animated.

All of the components of jQuery UI require the jQuery core library plus a CSS and a JavaScript file in order to work. The CSS file must be added to your HTML file before jQuery, and the JavaScript file must be added afterwards.

```
<head lang="en">
<meta charset="UTF-8">
<link rel="stylesheet" href="//code.jquery.com/ui/1.11.4/themes/
smoothness/jquery-ui.css">
<script src="//code.jquery.com/jquery-1.10.2.js"></script>
<script src="//code.jquery.com/ui/1.11.4/jquery-ui.js"></script>
<title>Chapter06-Forms</title>
```

The preceding markup shows how to correctly add jQuery UI support to a website. First, we add the CSS file, then jQuery, and finally we add jQuery UI.

> The preceding code is using a content delivery network, CDN, to host the files. You can also host the files on your own server, but by using a CDN, you can get a potential performance boost because user browsers may have already cached your files the first time they ever came to your site.

Once we have the jQuery library loaded, using the tooltip is pretty simple. We need to hook the jQuery document ready event and set up our tooltip during it.

```
// Hook the document ready event and
$(document).ready(function () {
    // bind the tooltip plugin to the document
    $(document).tooltip({
        show: {
            effect: "slideDown",
            delay: 150
        }
    });
});
```

In the preceding sample, we wait for the document ready event. In the event handler, we bind the tooltip to the document. This makes it available to our entire site. The final step is to add an animation. The tooltip can be customized to animate onto and off of the page. Here, we have the tooltip animate onto the page after a 150 millisecond delay. It uses the `slideDown` animation effect.

Placeholder

Another feature that modern browsers have that older ones lack is placeholder text. It is the slightly grayed text that appears inside of input elements and disappears once the user begins to type. Placeholders are important to forms. They provide the user with a hint about the format of the content unlike the `<label>` element, which is what kind of information is expected. The placeholder attribute has only been around since HTML5. There are still plenty of browsers lacking support for it.

In order to add support for the placeholder attribute to older browsers, we will again use a plugin, but not one from the jQuery team. Instead, we will use the excellent jquery-placeholder, from Mathias Bynens. It is available for download from both bower and npm, but we will download it directly from its GitHub repo at: `http://mathiasbynens.github.io/jquery-placeholder/`. Since we aren't concerned with how it works, only with how to use it, we will install the minified version in our site. In order to do that, we add the following line to our HTML file:

```
<script src="jquery.placeholder.min.js"></script>
```

The placeholder is a type of plugin referred to as a polyfill. This means that its goal is only to give a browser missing a standard feature that feature. And if the browser already supports that standard, it does nothing. In order to activate the plugin, we add it to the jQuery document ready event, the same way we did earlier with the tooltip.

```
// Hook the document ready event and
$(document).ready(function () {
    // bind the placeholder to the input & textarea elements
    $('input, textarea').placeholder();
});
```

Enabling and disabling elements

Elements in your form that are not valid should be disabled. A disabled element is usually shown dimmed-out with gray text. A disabled element can't be focused, doesn't respond to the user, and won't be sent when the form is submitted.

The odd thing about the disabled attribute is that its presence inside of an element disables it. It doesn't need to be set to `true` or `false`. In fact, setting it `true` or `false` has no effect. To disable the element, add the disabled attribute. To enable the element, remove the disabled attribute. Luckily, jQuery understands this odd behavior and takes care of this detail for us.

We can use the jQuery `.prop()` method to help us out. When we want to disable the element, we do the following:

```
$('#someId).prop('disabled', true);
```

And when we want to enable the element, we do the following:

```
$('#someId).prop('disabled', false);
```

In spite of the way things look, jQuery will do exactly what we said. The first line of code will add the disabled attribute to the element and the second will remove it. Here is a more full-featured snippet of code:

```
// disables/enable elements
$('#disableEnable').click(function (event) {
    var $ptr = $('#names > *');
    if ($ptr.prop('disabled')) {
        $ptr.prop('disabled', false);
        $(this).text('Disable Them');
    } else {
        $ptr.prop('disabled', true);
        $(this).text('Enable Them');
    }
});
```

We begin by wiring up an event listener for the click event of the `disableEnable` button. Once the event is received, we check to see if the button is currently disabled. If it is, we enable it and change the button's text label. If the element is not disabled, we disable it and change the text message.

Validation

So far, we've learned how to hook form events, how to provide modern browser features like placeholder and tooltips to older browsers, and how to use jQuery form methods to gather all of our form data. But we are not doing something really important: validating the data.

Validation is important both for the user and for us as the site's creators. For users, validation can be used to let them know how to correctly fill out the form. We can gently nudge them when they make a mistake instead of allowing them to submit a bad form and telling them afterwards that the form contained errors. As the site's maintainers, it can be frustrating to find an address in a field that should have a phone number. HTML5 added a lot of validation features to the web. Before we take a look at what jQuery has to offer, let's see what we get for free in a modern browser.

The first HTML5-added attribute that we will look at seems so simple and trivial it is a bit hard to imagine that it didn't exist already: `autofocus`. The `autofocus` attribute declares which form element should have the focus when the form is loaded. Before it existed, the user had to click an element in order to select it or we had to use a bit of jQuery code like the following:

```
// Hook the document ready event and
$(document).ready(function () {
    // Give the title select element the focus
    $('#title').focus();
});
```

With HTML5, the preceding code is replaced with:

```
<select id="title" name="title" autofocus>
```

The `autofocus` attribute declares that this element gets the focus. Only one element should have the attribute at any given time.

HTML5 also added to the number of `<input>` element types. Previously, the only available types were:

Type	Purpose
Button	A push-down button
Checkbox	A checkbox
File	File selection
Hidden	Not displayed but is submitted to server
Image	A graphical version of the submit button
Password	Text field with an obscured value
Radio	A radio button
Reset	Resets the form's content to the default values
submit	Submits the form
Text	Single line text field

HTML5 added the following new types of `<input>`:

Type	Purpose
Color	A color picker
Date	A date picker (no time)
datetime	A date/time picker for UTC
datetime-local	A date/time picker for the local time zone
email	An e-mail address
month	A month/year picker
number	A text field for a floating point number
range	A range slider
search	A text field for search strings
Tel	A text field for a telephone number
Time	A time picker with no time zone
url	A text field for a URL
week	A week/year picker

It is important to state that there is very little checking on the different types. As an example, the Tel type allows for the entry of characters that are not normally part of a telephone number. Three HTML5 attributes can help: `minlength`, `maxlength`, and `pattern`. The `minlength` attribute states the minimum number of characters that can be entered in order for the string to be considered valid. The `maxlength` attribute does the same except for the maximum number of characters. The final attribute is `pattern`; it states a regular expression that the inputted string is checked against. In order for the string to be considered valid, it must pass. Regular expressions are super-handy for validation purposes, but they can be tricky to write correctly. Be sure to thoroughly test any regular expression that you add to your site. I also highly recommend using a site that has recipes for popular validation. One such site is the very popular regular expression site at: `http://www.regular-expressions.info`.

HTML5 also adds a very simple but important validation attribute: required. The required attribute simply states that an input element must be filled out in order for the form to be considered valid. If it is left empty or filled but not valid, compliant browsers will flag the error when the user attempts to submit the form. Unfortunately, the error message and style vary per browser. So once again, if we really want to be in charge of our site's styling, we must turn to our good friend jQuery.

Validation is not part of jQuery or jQuery UI, but it is the primary function of the jquery-validate plugin. It is written and maintained by a member of the jQuery, jQuery UI, and QUnit teams, Jörn Zaefferer. It began in 2006 and is still being maintained today, making it one of the oldest jQuery plugins. The home of jquery-validate is: `http://jqueryvalidation.org/`. It can be downloaded as a zip file there or via bower or nuget package managers. The core of the plugin is in the file `jquery.validate.js`. It is all you need for most installations.

Once you have the plugin added to your script files, next you need to add the call to the validate method on the forms you would like to validate to your jQuery document ready event handler. In order to minimize validation, just enhancing what HTML5 provides, all you need to add is something like the following line:

```
$('#personalInfo').validate();
```

This line tells the plugin to validate the form named `personalInfo`. Nothing else further is required. The plugin will behave in accordance with the validation attributes you placed on your form elements, even with browsers that are not HTML5 compliant.

If you would like more customization, you will need to pass an initialization object to the plugin. The two most important properties are rules and messages. The rules property defines how the plugin will validate each form element. The messages property defines which message the plugin will display when an element fails validation. Here is the code for our validation sample:

```html
<!DOCTYPE html>
<html>
<head lang="en">
<meta charset="UTF-8">
<link rel="stylesheet" href="//code.jquery.com/ui/1.11.4/themes/
smoothness/jquery-ui.css">
<script src="//code.jquery.com/jquery-1.10.2.js"></script>
<script src="//code.jquery.com/ui/1.11.4/jquery-ui.js"></script>
<script src="jquery.validate.min.js"></script>
<script src="jquery.placeholder.min.js"></script>
<title>Chapter06-Forms</title>
<style type="text/css">
        .wider {
            display: inline-block;
            width: 125px;
            margin-right: 8px;
        }
        select {
            margin-right: 8px;
```

```
            }
        .error{
            color: red;
        }
</style>
</head>
<body>
<div>
<form id="personalInfo">
<fieldset>
<legend>Personal Info</legend>
<p>
<label for="title" class="wider">Greeting</label>
<select id="title" name="title" class="wider" autofocus>
<option selected></option>
<option>Mr.</option>
<option>Ms.</option>
<option>Miss</option>
<option>Mrs.</option>
<option>Dr.</option>
</select>
</p>
<p>
<label for="firstName" class="wider">First Name:</label>
<input id="firstName" name="firstName" class="wider" type="text"
title="Your first name"/>
</p>
<p>
<label for="lastName" class="wider">Last Name:</label>
<input id="lastName" name="lastName" class="wider" type="text"
title="Your last name"/>
</p>
<p>
<label for="password" class="wider">Password:</label>
<input id="password" name="password" class="wider" type="password"
title="Your password" title="Your password"/>
</p>
<p>
<label for="confirmPassword" class="wider">Confirm Password</label>
<input id="confirmPassword" name="confirmPassword" class="wider"
type="password"  title="Confirm your password"/>
</p>
<p>
<label for="email" class="wider">E-Mail:</label>
```

```
<input id="email" name="email" class="wider" type="email" title="Your
email address" placeholder="yourname@email.com" />
</p>
</fieldset>
<input type="reset" value="Reset" class="wider"/>
<input type="submit" value="Submit" class="wider"/>
</form>
</div>
```

In addition to adding the validate plugin, we need to include jQuery and since we are still using the jQuery tooltip and placeholder plugins, we include them as well. Next, we add a bit of inline CSS to give us a little style.

Our form is pretty standard except for one thing: we are no longer adding any inline validation attributes. Instead, we define the validation rules in the JavaScript object that we pass into the validation method, which we will see next:

```
<script type="text/javascript">
    (function () {
        "use strict";

        // Hook the document ready event and
        $(document).ready(function () {
            // bind the placeholder polyfill to the input +
            textarea elements
            $('input, textarea').placeholder();
            // bind the tooltip plugin to the document
            $(document).tooltip({
                show: {
                    effect: "slideDown",
                    delay: 150
                }
            });
```

The first part of this code sample is fairly straightforward. We bind to jQuery's ready event and then enable the placeholder polyfill and tooltips.

```
            // bind validation to the personalInfo form
            $('#personalInfo').validate({
                rules: {
                    title: {
                        required: true
                    },
                    firstName: {
                        required: true,
                        minlength: 5
```

```
            },
            lastName: {
                required: true,
                minlength: 5
            },
            password: {
                required: true,
                minlength: 5
            },
            confirmPassword: {
                required: true,
                minlength: 5,
                equalTo: '#password'
            },
            email: {
                required: true,
                email: true
            }
        },
```

In the rules property of the validation object, we pass the names of all the elements we wish to validate. We can tell the validator which elements are required, their minimum lengths, whether they should match another element, and so on. The validator can do much more than shown in the code, so be sure to read the documentation to learn more.

```
        messages: {
            title: "Please choose a title.",
            firstName: "Please enter your first name.",
            lastName: "Please enter your last name.",
            password: "Please create a password.",
            confirmPassword: {
                required: "Please confirm your password.",
                equalTo: "Your passwords must match."
            },
            email: "Please enter a valid email."
        },
        submitHandler: function(form) {
            alert('submit');
        }
    });
    });
    }());
</script>
</body>
</html>
```

In the message property of the validation object, we pass all of the messages we wish to display. Any element or state not defined here will simply be assigned a default validation error message, which in many cases may be sufficient.

The final property passed to the validation method is the submit handler. This is the method that is called once the user has successfully submitted his form. You must use the submit handler and not the jQuery submit handler.

Filtering out unwanted characters

It is our job as web developers to keep the user from doing something bad accidentally. Validation lets the user know when they've entered something wrong. Filtering helps keep the user from entering invalid characters. In order to filter characters being entered into a text field, we will need to hook two events: "keypress" and "paste".

```
// filters out unwanted characters
$('#alphaNumOnly').on('keypress paste', function (event) {
    // convert the keycode into a character
    var nextChar = String.fromCharCode(event.which);
    if(event.type === 'keypress'){
    // add it to the current input text string, the remove any
    bad chars via regex
    this.value = (this.value + nextChar).replace(/[^0-9|a-z|AZ]+/g,
    '');
}
    // let the browser know we've handled this event
    event.preventDefault();
    return false;
});
```

Hooking the `keypress` event allows us to see each key as it is pressed and decide whether or not we want this character in our text field. We hook the paste key to stop the user from cutting and pasting strings into our text field. Most of the work is done by the regular expression. It filters out everything except numbers and letters.

Summary

Forms are very important to most websites. They are the primary way in which our site's users communicate with the site. Helping our user to fill out our forms and making sure that the data we get is good. We've seen many of the ways that jQuery helps us with forms. The tooltip plugin helps us to add the tooltips to browsers lacking it and to style the tooltips to match our site's look. The placeholder polyfill gives the placeholder attribute to older browsers and quietly steps out of the way for browsers that already support it.

jQuery also provides us with easy ways to hook the submit, change, and other form events. These events also provide points to validate the data before we submit it or once it has changed.

In the next chapter, we will learn about Ajax and how jQuery makes it almost trivial to send and receive data from our server.

7
Talking to Your Server

In *Chapter 6, Better Forms with jQuery,* we learned how to let jQuery help us to make better forms for our users. Once a form is filled, we will need to use jQuery to send it back to its server and to get fresh data. We live in the world of single page, fluid apps. Most of the top sites on the Internet update the sections of the page that need to change seamlessly via Ajax. This is a better experience for users than the old-fashioned way of posting data via the submit button and loading a new page. jQuery is ready to help us here. We can use it to get fresh data on demand from our server.

In this chapter, we will cover the following topics:

- Life before jQuery
- How jQuery helps us today
- Helper methods
- Ajax events

In order to understand how jQuery can help us talk to our server, we should first take a step back and explore what life was like before jQuery. During this time, websites had two ways to send data to the server: the `<form>` and `<a>` tags.

Before jQuery

The HTML `<form>` tag is the element that sends data to the server. It has two attributes that deal with how it sends data to its server. First, there is the `method` attribute, which lets it specify how to send data back to its server. It has two possible values: `get` or `post`.

Set the `method` attribute to `get` and it sends the form data appended to the end of the request to the server page specified by the `action` attribute. The form will send the data from all enabled form elements that have a `name` element defined. The `get` method should only be used for small bits of insensitive data. All data sent via a `get` is visible from the URL bar of the browser.

Setting the method attribute to `post` is considered more secure than `get` since it sends its data within the message body so it is not visible in the query string; but don't be fooled into thinking that the data is secured, it is simply not as visible. The `post` should be your go-to method when you are sending new data to the server.

The `<form>` tag encloses all of the form data elements that will be sent to the server when the submit button is clicked. Keep in mind that only valid elements will be sent. In order to be valid, an element must be enabled and have a `name` attribute. The `name` attribute is the name the value will be given on the server. Unlike the `id` attribute, `name` values can be duplicated, but if they are duplicated within a form, it is up to you to figure out which is which.

Another, sometimes overlooked, way to send small amounts of information to the server was by setting query parameters of the `href` attribute of the `<a>` tag. Admittedly, it can only send small chunks of information, but it can be really useful when you need to send data from one page to the next.

Both the `<form>` and the `<a>` tags result in a page refresh, but it was possible to do Ajax before jQuery. Many people don't realize that Ajax has been possible in Microsoft browsers since the late 1990s. They were implemented using Microsoft's proprietary ActiveX objects, but the usefulness of this capability was not lost to other browser makers who made it an object of the browser, the `XMLHTTPRequest` object, or XHR for short.

Unfortunately, writing code to support this functionality was not easy. Like so many things we have seen in browser programming in the past, the different implementations of similar functions caused us developers to have to write a great deal of plumbing code before we could begin to write feature code. Let's see what jQuery brings to the Ajax party.

How jQuery helps us

One of the ways jQuery helps us is by taking the pain out of Ajax. Users no longer want to wait through cycles where they click submit, the page goes blank, then new content loads. Sites like Facebook, Gmail, and Twitter have shown users that the web can be very app-like. Although jQuery is a library and not a programming framework like AngularJS or Ember, it can easily enable the fetching and sending of server data without doing page reloads.

In order to demonstrate the code snippets in this chapter, you will have to set up a web server. However, setting up a web server is beyond the scope of this book. One easy way is to use an editor/IDE that includes a built-in web server. Two such editors are JetBrains WebStorm and Adobe's Brackets. Both are available for Windows, Mac OS X, and Linux.

Loading HTML – .load()

One the first things that we would like our website to be able to do is to load fresh HTML markup on the page. This is where the .load() method comes in handy. It uses Ajax to download HTML from a URL on your server and insert it onto the page at the indicated location. If you need to create a simple single-page app, this method makes it easy. Under the covers, .load() uses the HTTP GET method, which is the same method used by the browser when it loads HTML. Let's take a look at some code:

```
<!DOCTYPE html>
<html>
<head lang="en">
    <meta charset="UTF-8">
    <script src="//code.jquery.com/jquery-1.10.2.js"></script>
    <title>Chapter07-AJAX</title>
    <style type="text/css">
        .output-region {
            border: 2px dashed lightblue;
            width: 100%;
            height: 200px;
        }
    </style>
</head>
<body>
<div>
    <div class="output-region" id="outputRegion"></div>
    <form id="myForm">
        <select name="greeting">
            <option selected value="Mr.">Mr.</option>
            <option value="Mrs.">Mrs.</option>
            <option value="Ms.">Ms.</option>
            <option value="Miss">Miss.</option>
            <option value="Dr.">Dr.</option>
        </select>
```

```
            <input name="firstName" value="Abel"/>
            <!-- is disabled -->
            <input name="middleName" disabled value="Middle"/>
            <input name="lastName" value="Alpha"/>
            <!-- doesn't have a name attribute -->
            <input id="suffix" value="Suffix"/>
            <input name="age" value="42"/>
        </form>
        <div id="dataTransfer" style="display: none;"><hr/>Data transfer
    in progress...</div>
        <hr/>
        <button type="button" class="load-page" data-page="page1">Get Page
    1</button>
        <button type="button" class="load-page" data-page="page2">Get Page
    2</button>
        <button type="button" class="load-page" data-page="page3">Get Page
    3</button>
        <button type="button" id="get-javascript">Get JavaScript</button>
        <button type="button" id="get-json">Get JSON</button>
        <button type="button" id="get-get">Get Get Data</button>
        <button type="button" id="get-post">Get Post Data</button>
        <button type="button" id="jq-param">Create Param</button>
        <button type="button" id="serialize">Serialize</button>
        <button type="button" id="serializeArray">Serialize Array</button>
    </div>
    <script type="text/javascript">
        (function (window, $, undefined) {
            "use strict";

            // Hook the document ready event and
            $(document).ready(function () {
                // error display
                function showError(err) {
                    alert('ERROR: ' + err.status + ' - ' + err.
                    statusText);
                }

                function showJsonMessage(data, erase) {
                    if(erase){
                        $('#outputRegion').text("");
                    }
                    $('#outputRegion').append($("<div>").text(JSON.
                    stringify(data)));
                }
                // load new HTML markup code
                $('.load-page').click(function (event) {
                    var fileToLoad = $(this).attr("data-page") + ".html";
                    $('#outputRegion').load(fileToLoad);
                });
```

```
        });
    }());
</script>
</body>
</html>
```

The preceding code divides into three sections. The first section is everything in the `<head>` tag. The only things important here are that we load jQuery from an online repo and include some inline CSS to delineate where we will eventually inject markup and JSON data.

The next section is our HTML markup. We have a large `<div>` with the `id` of output-region that will hold the results of our code. In the `<form>` tag, there are a few form elements that will give the form some data. The last row of HTML is a series of buttons that will activate each of our code snippets.

The final section of the file is our JavaScript. Initially, we have only one function, but we will add more code as we progress through this chapter. Let's get started by examining the load-page click event handler.

We've seen lots of event handler code and there is nothing new here. The first three buttons each use this handler when clicked. The handler will get the `data-page` attribute of the clicked button. The `data-page` attribute tells the code which page to load and it is appended with the extension of `.html`. This is passed to the `.load()` method, which uses it to grab the new markup from the server and write it to the location specified by the selector. If the `.load()` successfully retrieves the HTML, it writes to the indicated selector, which in our case is the `<div>` with the ID of `outputRegion`.

Loading JSON Data – .getJSON()

The `.getJSON()` method loads JSON data from the passed URL and calls a success function with the returned data or an error object is passed to a failed function. Like most of the Ajax method in jQuery 1.5 and above, it also returns a jQuery promise.

 A promise is an object that represents the eventual results of an asynchronous operation. It can have one of three states: pending, fulfilled, and rejected. When it is first created and hasn't resolved yet, it has a state of pending. If the promise is resolved successfully, its state changes to fulfilled. If the promise fails, its state changes to rejected. Once a promise's state changes from pending, it is never changed again.

With the jQuery promise in hand, we chain a `then` function to the `$.getJSON` method. The `then` function takes two parameters. The first is a function to be called if the promise is fulfilled successfully. The second parameter is a function to be called if there is an error. If everything is all right, the JSON data is converted to a JavaScript object and passed to the `success` function and a message appears in an alert prompt; otherwise the contents of the error object are displayed.

```
// load JSON data
$('#get-json').click(function (event) {
    $.getJSON('data.json').then(function(data){
        alert(data.message);
    }, function(err){
        alert('ERROR:' + JSON.stringify(err));
    });
}0029;
```

Loading and executing JavaScript – getScript()

Most of the Ajax methods get some kind of data from the server. The `.getScript()` method is different. It retrieves JavaScript from the server, parses, and then executes it. Like the other Ajax methods, it returns a promise, but in this case the `success` function is not passed any data.

```
// load and run javascript
$('#get-javascript').click(function (event) {
    $.getScript('script.js').then(function () {
        alert("getScript() was successful.");
    }, function(err){
        alert('ERROR:' + JSON.stringify(err));
    });
});
```

The code that the `.getScript()` method loaded is still available after it executes, but there is no easy way to call the code again unless you keep a reference to it. In the example code, we assign the `incrementer` function to the window object so it can be called later.

```
// wrap the code in a function for information hiding
(function () {
    "use strict"

    // we show a message to the user
```

```
    alert("We're from another script file, trust us");

    // bind the function to the window global object so I can call it
if I need it.
    window.incrementer = (function () {
        var lastNum = 0;
        return function (num) {
            lastNum += num;
            return lastNum;
        }
    }());
}());
```

Reading and writing data: jQuery.get() and .jQuery.post()

The final two shorthand methods are the $.get() and $.post() methods. We will describe them together since both methods are shortcuts for the jQuery.ajax() method. Keep in mind that anything done with a shortcut method can also be done by calling $.ajax(). The shortcut methods take care of a lot of the drudge work of making ajax calls. Let's check out some code:

```
// load JSON via $.ajax
$('#get-get').click(function (event) {
    $.ajax({
     method: "GET",
     url: "data1.json",
     success: function (data) {
       showJsonMessage(data);
    });
});
```

This code loads the data using an HTTP GET method. The $.get() shortcut method allows us to rewrite this as:

```
// load JSON via $.get
$('#get-get').click(function (event) {
    $.get("data1.json", function (data) {
        showJsonMessage(data);
    });
});
```

We pass the $.get() method just two parameters: the URL of the data and a success function; we don't even bother to pass an error function handler. Remember that with no error handler, the browser will silently eat any errors. The preceding code demonstrates using the $.get() method with a callback function. Let's make things more interesting by demonstrating how to use promise chaining.

```
// load JSON via $.get with promise chaining
$('#get-get2').click(function (event) {
    $.get("data1.json").
        then(function (data) {
            showJsonMessage(data, true);
            return $.get("data2.json");
        }).
        then(function (data) {
            showJsonMessage(data);
            return $.get("data3.json");
        }).
        then(function (data) {
            showJsonMessage(data);
            return $.get("data4.json");
        }).
        then(function (data) {
            showJsonMessage(data);
        }, showError);
});
```

The preceding code makes four sequential calls to the server. Each call requests a different bit of JSON data, which it renders via the showJsonMethod() function. If any of the calls fails, the showError() function of the last then() method is called and no further Ajax requests are made. Each successful call returns the next call so it is able to chain the promises together.

One potential downside is that the calls are made sequentially. Most browsers can do at least two simultaneous HTTP requests and some can do more. If performance is a concern and the order of the calls doesn't, we could make all of the HTTP request at the same time and let the browser determine how many it can handle. Luckily, jQuery promises have a $.when() method. It accepts all of the promises that you wish to wait on as parameters. Once all of the promises have been either resolved or rejected, the .then() method is called. The data sent to each promise is sent as parameters in the same order the promises are listed in the .when() method.

```
// load JSON via $.get with concurrent promises
$('#get-con').click(function (event) {
    var data1 = $.get("data1.json"),
        data2 = $.get("data2.json"),
```

```
        data3 = $.get("data3.json"),
        data4 = $.get("data4.json");
    $.when(data1, data2, data3, data4).then(function(d1, d2, d3, d4){
        showJsonMessage(d1, true);
        showJsonMessage(d2);
        showJsonMessage(d3);
        showJsonMessage(d4);
    }, showError);
});
```

In the preceding code, the same four HTTP requests are made except now they are made at the same time. The order in which each call will return data is non-deterministic, but the code will wait until all four calls complete before moving on. If any call fails, the entire operation is considered to have failed and the failure method is called. This is different than when we called the code sequentially. Each HTTP request could return data, but once one failed, the failure method was called and no more requests were made.

So far, all of the requests have been made with the `$.get()` method; we've completely ignored the `$.post()` method. Not to worry, both methods are shortcuts for the `$.ajax()` method. We can use the `$.post()` in place of the `$.get()` method pretty much anywhere. So let's replace the `$.get()` method from the first demo.

```
// load JSON via $.post
,/. $('#get-post').click(function (event) {
    $.post("data1.json", function (data) {
        showJsonMessage(data, true);
    });
});
```

So if the methods can be exchanged for one another, why have both? To be fair, we haven't been using them the way they are intended. The four main HTTP verbs are get, post, put, and delete. Get is intended to retrieve one or more items from a database. Post is intended to create a new record in the database. Put is meant to update an existing record. And finally, delete removes a record from the database. Using the verbs correctly lies at the heart of RESTful service APIs, which is a bit off-topic for this book.

Helper methods

jQuery provides us with a few Ajax helper methods. There are only three functions and each of them is easy to use and eliminates some grunt work for us.

Creating query data – $.param()

An Ajax request usually encodes data to pass to the server in the form of a query string. A query string follows the URL and begins with a question mark "?". Each parameter consists of a name and a value separated by an equals sign. Generating the parameter data is not difficult, but there are a few encoding rules that need to be followed correctly, or your request may fail. The $.param() will encode our data into a query string format.

```
// converts an array of objects to an encoded query string
$('#jq-param').click(function (event) {
    var testData = [
        {name: "first", value: "Troy"},
        {name: "last", value: "Miles"},
        {name: "twitter", value: "@therockncoder"}
    ];
    var myParam = $.param(testData);
    $('#outputRegion').text(myParam);
});
```

In the preceding code, we encode an array of objects named testData. Each of the objects has a name and a value property. These properties will be the name and the value of the encode string. We passed the array to the $.param() method and store the resulting string in myParam, which we then write to the output <div>.

Note how the $.param() method takes care of the encoding for us. The third array parameter contains an at sign @, which is correctly encoded as %40. It will also encode other symbols and spaces. Such symbols must be encoded or your Ajax request will fail. Or worse, it may seem to work but send and store incorrect data.

The $.param() method is only necessary when you are creating URLs by hand. If you call the $.get() or $.post() methods and pass data to them, they will correctly encode and append to the URL or message body correctly.

Creating query data from a form – .serialize()

The next helper method, serialize(), is similar to the $.param() method except instead of passing it data, it uses the <form> tag indicated by the selector to pull data from all of the valid form elements.

```
$('#serialize').click(function (event) {
    var myParam = $('#myForm').serialize();
    $('#outputRegion').text(myParam);
});
```

The preceding code serializes all of the form elements in the `myForm` `<form>` tag when the Serialize button is clicked and renders them to the page. Remember that only valid form elements will be serialized. If an element is disabled or doesn't have a name attribute, it won't be serialized. This method allows you to substitute jQuery for old-fashioned HTML form submits.

Creating an object from form data – .serializeArray()

The final member of the Ajax helpers is the `.serializeArray()` method. Like the `.serialize()` method previously described, it gets its data from all of the form elements within the selector specified `<form>` tag. It only uses valid form elements, which must be enabled and have a name element. The difference between this method and the `.serialize()` method is the way the data is encoded. The `.serializeArray()` method encodes the form data as an array of JavaScript objects. Each object consists of a name and a value property. The name is the contents of the element's name attribute and the value is the element's value. We can substitute this method for the `.serialize()` method.

```
// serialze the form data as an array of objects
$('#serializeArray').click(function (event) {
    var myParam = $('#myForm').serializeArray();
    $('#outputRegion').text(JSON.stringify(myParam));
});
```

The results of a call to `.serializeArray()` is an array of JavaScript objects. We place the results in the variable `myParam`, which is sent to the JSON `stringify()` method so it can be displayed.

Ajax events

Sometimes, your application would like to know when various Ajax events occur. Perhaps your application would like to display an icon that indicates that data is being sent to or received from the server and hide the icon once the request is complete. Luckily, jQuery provides us with global Ajax events. These events make it possible to know when any Ajax activity starts, stops, sends data, errors out, or succeeds. These events are global so they must hook the document element. Let's add them to our current sample code.

```
var $doc = $(document);
// when an ajax request begins
$doc.ajaxStart(function () {
    console.info("<<<< Triggered ajax start handler.");
```

```
        $('#dataTransfer').show('fast');
    });
    // once all ajax request complete,
    $doc.ajaxStop(function () {
        console.info(">>>> Triggered ajax stop handler.");
        $('#dataTransfer').hide('slow');
    });
    // called at the beginning of each request
    $doc.ajaxSend(function (event, jqxhr, settings) {
        console.info("#### Triggered ajaxSend handler for: " + settings.
        url);
    });
    // called every time a request succeeds
    $doc.ajaxSuccess(function (event, jqxhr, settings) {
        console.info("#### Triggered ajaxSuccess handler for: " +
        settings.url);
    });
    // called every time a request fails
    $doc.ajaxError(function (event, jqxhr, settings) {
        console.info("#### Triggered ajaxError handler for: " + settings.
        url);
    });
    // called at the end of every request whether it succeeds or fails
    $doc.ajaxComplete(function (event, jqxhr, settings) {
        console.info("#### Triggered ajaxComplete handler for: " +
        settings.url);
    });
```

In the sample code, we hook three Ajax events: `ajaxStart`, `ajaxStop`, and `ajaxSend`.

When an Ajax request begins – .ajaxStart()

The `.ajaxStart()` method is triggered when the first Ajax request begins. If another request is already in progress, the event won't be fired. In the sample code, we make the hidden `<div>` with the message *Data transfer in progress…* visible in the handler for this event.

When an Ajax request completes – .ajaxStop()

The `.ajaxStop()` fires once all Ajax requests have finished. Like the `.ajaxStart()` method, it is smart enough to only fire when appropriate, allowing us to pair them together to hide and display the message.

When running the code locally, you will find that the stop event is fired very quickly after the start event. In order to allow the message to be seen, we send the hide method a parameter of slow. Without this parameter, it would be difficult for the user to read the message.

When an Ajax request sends data – .ajaxSend()

Before Ajax data is sent, the .ajaxSend() handler is called. If you need to differentiate which Ajax request triggered .ajaxSend(), it sends three parameters to your handler function: event, jqxhr, and settings. The settings parameter is an object that holds two important properties: url and type. The url property is a string hold the URL that the request is calling. The type is which HTTP verb the request is using. By checking these two properties, you should be able to determine which of your Ajax requests triggered the event.

When an Ajax request fails – .ajaxError()

If a request fails, the .ajaxError() handler will be fired. The jQuery XHR object, parameter jqxhr, will hold the error information. The status code will be in the status property and the error message will be in the statusText property.

When an Ajax request succeeds – .ajaxSuccess()

If the request succeeds, the .ajaxSuccess() handler will be fired. The jQuery XHR object will hold the status information. Again, the status code is in the status property and the status text is in the statusText property.

When an Ajax request finishes – .ajaxComplete()

The .ajaxComplete() handler is called whenever an Ajax request completes. This method is always called regardless of whether the request succeeded or failed. It is always called after the success or error event.

The order that events are called for a single request is always the same. First, the start event, then the send, followed by either the success or error event, then the complete event, and finally the stop event. If more than one request is made, the order that the events are fired becomes non-deterministic. The only thing that can be guaranteed is that the start is the first event and stop is the last.

Summary

Modern web apps must smoothly send and retrieve data to their servers. jQuery helps us interact seamlessly with our server and eliminates the need to do a full-page refresh.

In this chapter, we learned how to pull new data, JavaScript, and HTML from our server. Also, how to post data to the server without doing a page refresh. And we also learned about some helper methods that jQuery provides that make it easier for us to package our data properly for transmission.

One major criticism of jQuery isn't the library itself but the fact that applications written with it tend to quickly grow unruly. In the next chapter, we will look at ways we can keep our code from looking like spaghetti.

8
Writing Code that You can Read Later

jQuery truly does help us do more with less code, but one thing it doesn't address is how to organize our code. This may not be a problem at first, but as your app grows in age and features, it's organization (or lack thereof), becomes a problem.

In this chapter, we will look at some proven methods to organize JavaScript. In this chapter we will:

- Learn some object-oriented techniques to make our code easy to understand and maintain
- Use events to decouple our code and ensure that unrelated sections don't need to directly talk to each other
- Take a quick look at writing JavaScript unit testing, specifically with Jasmine, which is a behavior-driven development framework used to test JavaScript code

Separation of concerns

Software architectural patterns, such as **Model-View-Controller** (**MVC**), have become popular mainly because they address the issue of code organization head-on. Model-View-Controller divides an application into three main parts. The model is the part that deals with the application's data. The controller gets the data from the model and feeds it to the view, and it takes user input from the view and feeds it back to the model. One of the most important things about this pattern is that you should never mix responsibilities. The model never contains the controller code, the controller never contains views, and so on. This is called **Separation of Concerns**, or SoC. If any part of the application violates this rule, your application will descend into a hot mess of tightly coupled, interdependent code.

We don't need to go all in with MVC in order to gain some benefits from it. We can use it as a way to guide us in our development. For one, it helps us answer this question: where should this code go? Let's look at an example. We are given the requirement to write the code to retrieve membership data from our web service and render it for the user to select from. How should we proceed? Your first impulse might be to write some code like the following:

```html
<!DOCTYPE html>
<html>
<head lang="en">
  <meta charset="UTF-8">
  <script src="//code.jquery.com/jquery-1.10.2.js"></script>
  <title>Chapter08-Clean Code</title>
</head>
<body>
<div>Super Coding Club Members</div>
<hr/>
<ul id="myList"></ul>
<hr/>

<script type="text/javascript">
  // Hook the document ready event and
  $(document).ready(function () {
    // get the user data
    $.getJSON('users.json', function (members) {
      var index, htmlTemplate = '';
      // make sure there are some members
      if (members && members.length) {
        // create the markup
        for (index = 0; index < members.length; index += 1) {
          htmlTemplate += '<li>' + members[index].name.first +
          '</li>';
        }
        // render the member names
        $('#myList').html(htmlTemplate);
      }
      return members;
    }).fail(function (error) {
      alert("Error: " + error.status + ": " + error.statusText);
    });
  });
</script>
</body>
</html>
```

This code achieves our requirements but has several problems. First, there is no separation of concerns. While we are not striving to create an MVC application, we should at least strive to have functions that are broken down along model, view, and controller lines. Our model, in this case, is represented by the $.getJSON() method call. It is bound directly to our controller code, which takes the model data and creates an HTML template out of it in this example. And finally, our view code takes the HTML template and renders it using a $.html() method.

This code is also an example of tight coupling. Each section of the code depends directly on the next, and there is no way to pull them apart. Tightly coupled code is more difficult to test. There is no easy way to test this code's functionality. Just look at it. The code is inside the document-ready event; you would have to mock that event in order to even begin testing the code's functionality. Once you've mocked the document-ready event, you will also need to somehow mock the getJSON() method since the rest of the code is buried inside it.

Breaking code into logical units

One of the things that makes the previous code sample hard to understand is that it hasn't been broken down into logical units. In JavaScript, we don't have classes like other object-oriented languages, but we have objects and even files to keep logically related units of code together.

We break code down, starting with the functions. Rather than having one function that does everything, strive to have many functions, with each function only doing one thing. When functions do too many things, they become hard to understand. Comments may help explain what the code is doing, but well-written code should comment itself. Functions help clearly separate the different bits of functionalities.

You may be wondering why any of this matters, especially since we have working code that achieves our requirements. It matters since the typical program spends far more time being maintained than written. So, it is important that we write our code to be maintainable. Let's try this again:

```
<script type="text/javascript">
  function showHttpError(error) {
    alert("Error: " + error.status + ": " + error.statusText);
  }

  function getMembers(errorHandler) {
    return $.getJSON('users.json').fail(errorHandler);
  }
```

```
function createMemberMarkup(members) {
  var index, htmlTemplate = '';
  members.forEach(function (member) {
    htmlTemplate += '<li>' + member.name.first + '</li>';
  });
  return htmlTemplate;
}

function renderMembers($ptr, membersMarkup) {
  $ptr.html(membersMarkup);
}

function showMembers() {
  getMembers(showHttpError)
    .then(function (members) {
      renderMembers($('#members'), createMemberMarkup(members));
    });
}

// Hook the document ready event
$(document).ready(function () {
  showMembers();
});
</script>
```

The second version of the code is longer than the original, and even though it lacks comments, it is more legible. Separating the code into separate functions makes it easy to understand what it is doing.

In a complete MVC application, we might create separate classes for each concern and then move each function into the class to which it belongs. But we don't need to be so formal. First, we don't have classes in JavaScript, but we have very powerful objects that can contain functions. So let's try again, using a JavaScript object to bundle up our code this time:

```
<script type="text/javascript">
  var members = {
      showHttpError: function (error) {
        alert("Error: " + error.status + ": " + error.statusText);
      },
```

```
      get: function (errorHandler) {
        return $.getJSON('users.json').fail(errorHandler);
      },

      createMarkup: function (members) {
        var index, htmlTemplate = '';
        members.forEach(function (member) {
          htmlTemplate += '<li>' + member.name.first + '</li>';
        });
        return htmlTemplate;
      },

      render: function ($ptr, membersMarkup) {
        $ptr.html(membersMarkup);
      },

      show: function () {
        var that = this;
        that.get(that.showHttpError)
          .then(function (members) {
            that.render($('#members'), that.createMarkup(members));
          });
      }
    };

    // Hook the document ready event
    $(document).ready(function () {
      members.show();
    });
  </script>
```

In this version, we have all our code bundled into the member object. This makes it easy to move our code about and helps us think of it as a single, cohesive unit. Putting the code into an object also makes it possible to use the `this` construct. It is arguable whether it is an improvement or not. I've seen many a JavaScript developer type all object names out in the long form just to avoid having to think about this. Note that we also shorten most of the method names. Having the word `member` in many of the method names is redundant since the name of object is `member`. Also, note that we are now calling our functions "methods". When a function is part of a class or object, it is a method.

Using events to decouple code

Through this book, we have used events, but they have always been triggered by jQuery or the browser but never by us. Now, that is about to change. Events are really great for the decoupling of code. Imagine a scenario where you and another developer are working together on an application. The other developer is going to supply your code with data. This data—let's call it the data source—will be available intermittently, unlike the previous example of supplying the data via a single Ajax call. Your code, the data reader, will render the data to the page when it becomes available. There are several ways that we could go about this.

The data source could provide a polling method for us to call. We would repeatedly call this method until the source has some new data for us. However, we know that polling is inefficient. The majority of the time we call the polling service, there won't be any new data, and we will have burned CPU cycles without returning any new data.

We could supply the data source with a method it could call whenever it has new data. This solves the issue of inefficiency since our code will only be called when there is new data. Think about what a maintenance nightmare we would introduce by doing this. When there is only one dependent module that the data source is supplying data to, it seems easy enough. But what if a second or third module also needs the data source? We will have to keep updating the data source module. And if any of the data reader modules change, the data source may need to be updated as well. What should we do?

We can use custom events. Using custom events loosens the coupling. Neither side directly calls the other. Instead, when the data source has new data, it triggers the custom event. Any data reader that wants the new data simply registers a handler for the custom events.

Here are some of the nice things about using custom events. First, the coupling is loose. Second, there is no limit to the number of data readers that can register for the event. Third, if the event is triggered with no listeners, nothing breaks. And finally, if there is a bunch of readers registered but new data never comes, nothing breaks.

One thing we must be careful about with custom events is to remember to release the event handlers when we are through with them. Two things can happen if we forget. First, we may cause a memory leak. A memory leak is when JavaScript is unable to release a chunk of memory because something—in our case, an event handler—is still holding a reference to it.

Over time, the browser will begin to act increasingly sluggish as it begins to run out of memory before it finally crashes. Second, our event handler can be called too many times. This happens when the code that hooks the event is called more than once without the event ever being released. Before you know it, the event handler is called two times, three times, or more instead of being called only once.

One last nice thing about custom events is that we already know most of what we need to in order to implement them. The code is only slightly different from what we learned in order to perform regular browser events. Let's take a look at a simple example first:

```html
<!DOCTYPE html>
<html lang="en">
<head>
  <meta charset="UTF-8">
  <script src="../libs/jquery-2.1.1.js"></script>
  <title>Chapter 8 Simple Custom Events</title>
</head>
<body>
<button id="eventGen">Trigger Event</button>
<button id="releaseEvent">Release Event Handlers</button>
<div id="console-out" style="width: 100%">
</div>

<script>
  var customEvent = "customEvent";

  function consoleOut(msg){
    console.info(msg);
    $('#console-out').append("<p>" + msg + "</p>");
  }

  function customEventHandler1(eventObj) {
    return consoleOut("Custom Event Handler 1");
  }

  function customEventHandler2(eventObj) {
    return consoleOut("Custom Event Handler 2");
  }

  $(document).ready(function () {
```

```
    // Notice we can hook the event before it is called
    $(document).on(customEvent, customEventHandler1);
    $(document).on(customEvent, customEventHandler2);

    // generate a new custom event for each click
    $('#eventGen').on('click', function () {
      $.event.trigger(customEvent);
    });
    // once we release the handlers, they are not called again
    $('#releaseEvent').on('click', function () {
      consoleOut("Handlers released");
      $(document).off(customEvent, customEventHandler1);
      $(document).off(customEvent, customEventHandler2);
    });
  });
</script>
</body>
</html>
```

In this example, we place two buttons on the page. The first button triggers an event, and the second one releases the event handlers. Below the buttons is a wide `<div>` that is used to display messages.

The code inside the script tags first creates a variable named `customEvent`, which holds the name of the custom event. The name of the event is up to you, but I would suggest something that includes your company's reverse domain name since you wouldn't want a future browser release to break your code because it uses the same event name. Then, we have the two event handlers that don't do anything particularly interesting.

Finally, in the document-ready event handler, we hook the custom event twice. We use the click event of the first button to trigger the custom event and the click event of the second button to release the handlers.

One thing we didn't show in this example was how to pass data to the custom event handler code. Luckily, this isn't difficult, so let's show how with another example:

```
<!DOCTYPE html>
<html lang="en">
<head>
  <meta charset="UTF-8">
  <script src="../libs/jquery-2.1.1.js"></script>
  <title>Chapter 8 Custom Events 2</title>
</head>
```

```
<body>
<div> <button id="stop">Stop Polling</button> <span
id="lastNewUser"></span></div>
<hr/>
<div id="showUsers">
</div>
<script>
  var users = [];
  var newUser = "com.therockncoder.new-user";
  function showMessage(msg) {
    $('#lastNewUser').show().html(msg + ' welcome to the
    group!').fadeOut(3000);
  }
    function init() {
    function getUserName(user) {
      return user.name.first + " " + user.name.last;
    }
    function showUsers(users) {
      var ndx, $ptr = $('#showUsers');
      $ptr.html("");
      for (ndx = 0; ndx < users.length; ndx += 1) {
        $ptr.append('<p>' + getUserName(users[ndx]) + '</p>')
      }
    }
    function addNewNameToList(eventObj, user, count) {
      console.info("Add New Name to List = " + getUserName(user));
      users.push(user);
      showUsers(users);
    }
    function welcomeNewUser(eventObj, user) {
      var name = getUserName(user);
      showMessage(name);
      console.info("got New User " + name);
    }
    $(document).on(newUser, addNewNameToList);
    $(document).on(newUser, welcomeNewUser);
  }
  function startTimer() {
    init();
    var handleId = setInterval(function () {

$.getJSON('http://api.randomuser.me/?format=json&nat=us').
success(function (data) {
```

```
      var user = data.results[0].user;
      $.event.trigger(newUser, [user]);
    });
  }, 5000);
  $('#stop').on('click', function(){
    clearInterval(handleId);
    showMessage('Cancelled polling');
  });
}
$(document).ready(startTimer);
</script>
</body>
</html>
```

Let's walk through the code to make sure we understand what it is doing.

The user interface consists of a single button labeled **stop** and a horizontal rule. Members will appear below the horizontal rule, and messages will appear next to the button.

Inside the script tags, the code kicks off by creating an empty array for the users and a string to hold the name of our custom events. The code consists of three main functions: showMessage, init, and startTimer. When the document-ready event fires, it calls the init method and then the startTimer method.

The startTimer method makes repeated calls every 5 seconds to a random user web service. It gives us a random new user every time it is called. In the init method, we establish two handlers for our custom event: addNewNameToList and welcomeNewUser. Each method takes the user data that the event provides and does something different with it. To stop the example program, click on the **stop** button and it will clear the interval timer.

Using unit tests

Unit tests are a funny subject. It seems that everyone agrees that it is good to write tests, but few people actually do it. A complete examination of unit testing would take an entire book but, hopefully, we can cover just enough about unit tests to show you how to add them to your code and explain why you should.

My preferred unit test framework is Jasmine, `http://jasmine.github.io/`. This is not to slight any of the other fine frameworks available, but Jasmine works on the frontend and backend, works in the browser and the command line, is actively maintained, and does all one would want from a test framework. Keep in mind that while the code is written for Jasmine, the principles can be applied to any JavaScript unit test framework. Before we look into how to write unit tests, we should begin with why we should write unit tests at all.

Why write unit tests at all?

In the beginning, JavaScript was rarely used in websites. When it was used, it was only to do minor things that could live without if JavaScript was disabled. So, the list of things was small, mainly client-side form validation and simple animations.

Nowadays, things have changed. Many sites won't run at all with JavaScript disabled. Others will run with limited functionality and usually display a missing JavaScript warning. So since we rely so heavily on it, it makes sense to test it.

We write unit tests for three main reasons: to verify that our application is functioning correctly, to verify that it continues to work correctly after the modification, and finally, to guide our development when using either **Test Driven Development (TDD)** or **Behavior Driven Development (BDD)**. We are going to focus on the first point, verifying that our application is functioning correctly. We will use the Jasmine Behavior-Driven JavaScript testing framework to do that. Jasmine runs from either the command line or from the browser. We will only use it from the browser.

In order to keep our example short, we will run the quintessential unit test example: an arithmetic calculator. It will be able to add, subtract, multiply, and divide two numbers. To test the calculator, we will need three files: `SpecRunner.html`, `calculator.js`, and `calculator-spec.js`. `SpecRunner.html` loads the other two files and the Jasmine framework. Here is the `SpecRunner.html` file:

```
<!DOCTYPE html>
<html>
<head>
  <meta charset="utf-8">
  <title>Jasmine Spec Runner v2.2.0</title>
  <!-- Jasmine files -->
  <link rel="shortcut icon" type="image/png"
  href="../libs/jasmine-2.3.4/jasmine_favicon.png">
```

```html
    <link rel="stylesheet" href="../libs/jasmine-2.3.4/jasmine.css">
    <script src="../libs/jasmine-2.3.4/jasmine.js"></script>
    <script src="../libs/jasmine-2.3.4/jasmine-html.js"></script>
    <script src="../libs/jasmine-2.3.4/boot.js"></script>

    <!-- System Under Test -->
    <script src="calculator.js"></script>

    <!-- include spec files here... -->
    <script src="spec/calculator-spec.js"></script>
</head>
<body>
</body>
</html>
```

There is nothing particularly challenging in `SpecRunner.html`. Besides the files that Jasmine needs in order to run, you place your application — not all of it, only the parts required for the unit tests to be able to run and the unit test files. By tradition, the unit test files have the same name as the file that they are testing, with `-spec` added to the end.

Here is the `calculator.js` file:

```javascript
var calculator = {
  add: function(a, b){
    return a + b;
  },
  subtract: function(a, b){
    return a -b;
  },
  multiply: function(a, b){
    return a * b;
  },
  divide: function(a, b){
    return a / b;
  }
};
```

Our calculator is simple and easy to understand. It is a JavaScript that has four functions: add, subtract, multiply, and divide. Testing its functionality should be equally simple, and it actually is. Here is the `spec` file that tests the calculator:

```
describe("Calculator", function() {

  it("can add numbers", function(){
    expect(calculator.add(12, 3)).toEqual(15);
    expect(calculator.add(3000, -100)).toEqual(2900);
  });

  it("can subtract numbers", function(){
    expect(calculator.subtract(12, 3)).toEqual(9);
  });

  it("can multiply numbers", function(){
    expect(calculator.multiply(12, 3)).toEqual(36);
  });

  it("can divide numbers", function(){
    expect(calculator.divide(12, 3)).toEqual(4);
  });
});
```

Jasmine's unit test framework works around three methods: `describe`, `it`, and `expect`. The `describe` is a global function that holds a test suite. Its first parameter is a string holding the name of the test suite. The second parameter is a function that is the test suit. Next up is `it`.

Like `describe`, `it` is a global function in Jasmine, and `it` holds a specification, or spec. The parameters passed to `it` are also a string and a function. By tradition, the string is written so that when read with `it`, it completes a sentence describing the specification. The function performs the test using one or more expectations.

Expectations are created using the `expect` Jasmine function. The `expect` is the equivalent of `assert` in other unit test frameworks. It is passed a single parameter, which is the value to be tested that calls the actual in Jasmine. Chained to the expectation is the `matcher` function. The `matcher` function is passed the expected value.

The combination of the `expect` and `matcher` functions in Jasmine is one of its most beautiful things. When written correctly, they read like an English sentence. This makes it easy to both write tests and read them later. Jasmine also comes with a large number of matchers, which helps you to write exactly the expectation you want. There is also a `not` operator that will reverse the logic of any `matcher  function`.

In order to run the sample test, simply launch the `SpecRunner.html` page. It will load Jasmine, the parts of code we would like to test, and the specifications. In unit test tradition, the page will either be green, which means all of our specifications have passed, or red, which means that at least one specification has failed.

Jasmine's goal is to help us find and fix broken tests. If, for instance, our add specification failed, we would see the name of the test suite and the failing specification displayed together in red: "Calculator can add numbers." Below it would be the failing expectations. It would show us what value it had and what value we expected.

In the sample code, we create our test suite with a call to the `describe` method. We have specifications, each testing one aspect of our calculator. Note how have worded our specifications so that they read like sentences. Our first specification reads "it can add numbers". When our test passes, we'll see the test suite display the word "Calculator" and each of the specifications listed below it, stating with what was tested.

Jasmine also has `setup` and `teardown` functions. A `setup` function executes before each specification in a test suite runs. A `teardown` function runs after each specification runs. We haven't used either in the sample code, but they can be quite useful in more complicated tests, especially when objects need to be prepared and cleaned up afterward.

Jasmine is a complete unit test framework. We've barely scratched the surface of what it can do. Also, keep in mind that while running Jasmine from the browser is convenient, more power comes from running it from the command line. Then, it is able to integrate into you website's build process. But this is only an introduction; to fully appreciate how Jasmine can help you write cleaner and also help you test jQuery, you will need to try it in your code.

Summary

We covered a lot of ideas in this chapter. Developers often forget that JavaScript is an object-oriented language, but it is not a class-based language. One of the most important things to keep in mind is the technique of Separation of Concerns. It is the cornerstone of keeping your code understandable and maintainable. Learning about SoC led us to the topics of breaking our code into logical units and using events to decouple our code. We ended the chapter by learning how to unit test our code with the popular open source tool, Jasmine.

Now that we've learned how to organize our code, it is time for us to turn our attention to other things people complain about in relation to jQuery: performance. In the next chapter, we will learn how to measure the performance of our code and the simple things we can do to speed it up. Quite a few blog posts have made it seem that jQuery is to blame for the slowness of many websites. If you don't understand JavaScript or jQuery well, it is easy to reach this conclusion. Luckily, it is not difficult to learn a few rules of thumb that can dramatically improve the speed of your jQuery code.

9
Faster jQuery

jQuery's detractors have two legitimate complaints against it. The first complaint is that jQuery creates hard-to-read, spaghetti code. In the previous chapter, we addressed this complaint by showing how to write code that is both easy to read and maintain. The second complaint is that jQuery creates slow code. This, too, is a legitimate complaint. The problem with jQuery or any other library is that if you don't understand it, it is easy to choose the wrong way to do something. In this chapter, we will address the second complaint: slow jQuery code.

To be sure, jQuery itself is written in highly performance-tuned JavaScript; in fact, I highly recommend that you study its source code. The problem with performance and jQuery is usually one of not understanding how it works. It is this lack of understanding that causes programmers to write inefficient code. But thankfully, jQuery is not that hard to understand, and when we pair this understanding with performance measuring tools, we can easily improve the performance of our code.

In this chapter, we will:

- Learn how to measure the speed of our JavaScript code
- Measure the performance of different jQuery snippets
- Learn when not to use jQuery and use plain vanilla JavaScript instead

Writing performance tests

Before we worry about how to improve our app's performance, we should first learn how to measure it. Simply saying "the app feels sluggish" isn't enough. In order to improve an app's performance, you must be able to measure it before you can improve it. Luckily for us, there have been many improvements in our browsers in the past few years. One such improvement is the User Timing API. It isn't officially part of all browsers since it is only a recommendation of the W3C, but it is supported by modern versions of all of the major browsers except Safari. We won't deploy our measuring code with our app, so the lack of Safari support, while regretful, isn't a deal killer.

I know some are wondering why we need a new way to measure time. We've had `Date.now()` since the introduction of ECMAScript 5.1 in 2009 and `new Date().getTime()` before that. The problem is one of resolution; at best, `Date.now()` can measure with an accuracy of 1 millisecond, which simply isn't good enough. The computer can execute a lot of JavaScript instructions in 1 millisecond.

The User Timing API is easy to use. We aren't going to explain all of its capabilities. We will only show just enough to help us write our performance-measuring code. The first function we need to get to know is `performance.now()`. It is similar to `Date.now()` in that it returns the current system time, but it differs in two important ways: first, it returns a floating point value, not an integer value like `Date.now()`. The floating-point value represents a precision of 1 microsecond or one-thousandths of a millisecond. Second, `performance.now()` is monotonically increasing, which is a fancy way of saying that it always increases. This means that whenever it is called consecutively, the value of the second call is always greater than the first. This is something that is not guaranteed with `Date.now()`. It might seem strange, but `Date.now()` is not monotonically increasing. `Date.now()` is based on time, and most systems have a process that keeps time in sync by adjusting `Date.now()` by a few milliseconds every 15 or 20 minutes. Because the resolution of `Date.now()` is a millisecond at best, anything that happens in less time than it gets rounded down to 0. A simple example will help explain the problem better:

```
function dateVsPerformance() {
  var dNow1 = Date.now();
  var dNow2 = Date.now();
  var pNow1 = performance.now();
  var pNow2 = performance.now();

  console.info('date.now elapsed: ' + (dNow2 - dNow1));
  console.info('performance.now elapsed: ' + (pNow2 - pNow1));
}
```

The preceding code is pretty straightforward. We make two consecutive calls to both `Date.now()` and `performance.now()`, which then display the elapsed time. In most browsers, the elapsed time of `Date.now()` will be zero, which we instinctively know can't be true. It doesn't matter how fast your computer is; it will always take some amount of time to execute every instruction. The problem is the resolution: `Date.now()` operates with a millisecond resolution and JavaScript instructions take microseconds to execute.

  1 millisecond equals 1,000 microseconds.

Luckily, `performance.now()` has a microsecond resolution; it always shows a difference between any two calls. When called consecutively, it will usually be at the submillisecond level.

`Performance.now()` is a very useful method, but it is not the only tool in the performance toolbox. The creators of the User Timing API realized that most of us were going to measure our app's performance, so they wrote methods to make it easier. First, there is the `performance.mark()` method; when passed a string, it will internally store the value of `performance.now()` using the passed string as a key:

```
performance.mark('startTask1');
```

The preceding code stores a performance mark with the name `startTask1`.

Next, there is `performance.measure()`. It will create a named timing measurement. It has three strings as parameters. The first string is the name of the measurement. The second string is the name of the starting performance mark, and the final string is the name of the ending performance mark:

```
performance.measure('task', 'startTask1', 'endTask1');
```

The User Timing API will store the measurement internally with the name as a key. In order to see our performance measures, we simply need to ask for them. The simplest way is to ask for all of them and then loop through them to display each one. The following code demonstrates the technique:

```
<!DOCTYPE html>
<html>
<head lang="en">
  <meta charset="UTF-8">
  <script src="//code.jquery.com/jquery-1.10.2.js"></script>
```

```
    <title>Chapter09 - User Timing API</title>
  </head>
  <body>
  <script>
    function showMeasurements() {
      console.log('\n');
      var entries = performance.getEntriesByType('measure');
      for (var i = 0; i < entries.length; i++) {
        console.log('Name: ' + entries[i].name +
          ' Start Time: ' + entries[i].startTime +
          ' Duration: ' + entries[i].duration + '\n');
      }
    }
    function delay(delayCount) {
      for (var ndx = 0; ndx < delayCount; ndx++) {
      }
    }
    function init() {
      performance.mark('mark1');
      delay(1000);
      performance.mark('mark2');
      delay(10);
      performance.mark('mark3');
      performance.measure('task1', 'mark1', 'mark2');
      performance.measure('task2', 'mark2', 'mark3');
      showMeasurements();
      performance.clearMeasures();
    }
    $(document).ready(init);
  </script>
  </body>
  </html>
```

 The preceding code displays all of its results to the browser console; nothing is displayed to the document.

The action begins with the code hooking the document-ready event, which calls the `init()` function. A call to `performance.mark()` is made to create a mark for `mark1`. We then call `delay()` with a counter value of 1,000 to simulate the performance of a useful task and then follow with another call to `performance.mark()`, which creates another performance marker, `mark2`. Again, we call `delay()`, this time with a smaller counter of 10 and create another performance marker, `mark3`.

We now have three performance markers. In order to determine how long each simulated task took, we will need to measure the markers using the `performance.measure()` method. It takes three parameters: the name of the measurement, the name of the initial marker, and the name of the final marker. Each measurement will be recorded and stored internally in the performance object. In order to view the measurements, we call the `showMeasurements()` methods.

The `showMeasurements()` method begins by calling `performance.getEntriesByType('measure')`. This method returns an array holding all of the performance measures recorded by the performance object. Each item in the array is an object that contains the performance measurement's name, start time, and duration. It also contains its performance type, but we aren't displaying it.

The last thing we do is make a call to `performance.clearMeasures()`. Keep in mind that the performance object stores all of the marks and measures internally. If you don't clear them occasionally, your lists of measure might become ungainly long. When `performance.clearMeasures()` is called with no parameters, it clears all of the measures it has saved. It can also be called with the name of a measure to clear. You can just as easily clear marks that have been saved by calling `performance.clearMarks()`. Calling it with no parameters clears all the saved marks, and calling it with the name of a mark clears the mark.

Measuring jQuery

Now that we have a way to measure the JavaScript performance, let's measure some jQuery:

```
<!DOCTYPE html>
<html>
<head lang="en">
  <meta charset="UTF-8">
  <link
  href="//maxcdn.bootstrapcdn.com/bootstrap/3.3.2/
  css/bootstrap.min.css" rel="stylesheet"/>
  <script
  src="//ajax.googleapis.com/ajax/libs
  /jquery/2.1.1/jquery.js"></script>
  <script
  src="//maxcdn.bootstrapcdn.com/bootstrap/3.3.2
  /js/bootstrap.min.js"></script>
  <title>Chapter 9 - Measure jQuery</title>
</head>
<body>
```

```
<nav class="navbar navbar-inverse navbar-fixed-top">
  <div class="container">
    <div class="navbar-header">
      <button type="button" class="navbar-toggle collapsed" data-
      toggle="collapse" data-target="#navbar"
              aria-expanded="false" aria-controls="navbar">
        <span class="sr-only">Toggle navigation</span>
        <span class="icon-bar"></span>
        <span class="icon-bar"></span>
        <span class="icon-bar"></span>
      </button>
      <a class="navbar-brand" href="#">Measuring jQuery</a>
    </div>
    <div id="navbar" class="navbar-collapse collapse">
      <form class="navbar-form navbar-right">
        <div class="form-group">
          <input type="text" placeholder="Email" class="form-
          control">
        </div>
        <div class="form-group">
          <input type="password" placeholder="Password"
          class="form-control">
        </div>
        <button type="submit" class="btn btn-success">Sign
        in</button>
      </form>
    </div>
  </div>
</nav>
```

There's nothing tricky in the preceding code, really. It uses Bootstrap and jQuery to create a navigation bar. The nav bar isn't fully functional; it just makes our jQuery code follow some markup to parse:

```
<!-- Main jumbotron for a primary marketing message or call to
action -->
<div class="jumbotron">
  <div class="container">
    <h1>Chapter 9</h1>

    <p>This is a template for a simple marketing or informational
    website. It includes a large callout called a
```

```
     jumbotron and three supporting pieces of content. Use it as
     a starting point to create something more
     unique.</p>


     <p><a class="btn btn-primary btn-lg" href="#"
     role="button">Learn more "</a></p>
   </div>
 </div>

 <div class="container">
   <!-- Example row of columns -->
   <div class="row">
     <div class="col-md-4 bosco">
       <h2>First</h2>


       <p>I am the first div. Initially I am the on the left side
       of the page. </p>


       <p><a class="btn btn-default" href="#" role="button"
       name="alpha">View details "</a></p>
     </div>
     <div id="testClass" class="col-md-4 ">
       <h2>Second</h2>


       <p>I am the second div. I begin in-between the other two
       divs. </p>


       <p><a id='find-me' class="btn btn-default find-me" href="#"
       role="button" name="beta">View details "</a></p>
     </div>
     <div class="col-md-4">
       <h2>Third</h2>


       <p>I am the third div. Initially I am on the right side of
       the page</p>


       <p><a class="btn btn-default" href="http://www.google.com"
       role="button" name="delta">View details "</a></p>
     </div>
   </div>

 <hr>
 <form class="myForm">
```

```html
<div class="input-group">
  <select id="make" class="form-control">
    <option value="buick">Buick</option>
    <option value="cadillac">Cadillac</option>
    <option value="chevrolet">Chevrolet</option>
    <option value="chrysler">Chrysler</option>
    <option value="dodge">Dodge</option>
    <option value="ford">Ford</option>
  </select>
</div>
<div class="input-group">
  <select id="vehicleOptions" multiple class="form-control">
    <option selected value="airConditioning">air
    conditioning</option>
    <option value="cdPlayer">CD player</option>
    <option selected value="satelliteRadio">satellite
    radio</option>
    <option value="powerSeats">power seats</option>
    <option value="navigation">navigation</option>
    <option value="moonRoof">moon roof</option>
  </select>
</div>
<div class="input-group">
  <label for="comments" class="">Comments:</label>
  <textarea id="comments" class="form-control"></textarea>
</div>
<div class="input-group">
  <input type="text" id="firstName" class="form-control"
  placeholder="first name" value="Bob"/>
  <input type="text" id="lastName" class="form-control"
  value="" placeholder="last name"/>
</div>
</form>
<hr>

<footer>
  <p>© Company 2015</p>
</footer>
</div>
```

The preceding markup is the main content. Again, we are just giving ourselves some meaty HTML to parse through:

```
<script type="text/javascript">
  function showMeasurements() {
    console.log('\n');
    var entries = performance.getEntriesByType('measure');
    for (var i = 0; i < entries.length; i++) {
      console.log('Name: ' + entries[i].name +
        ' Duration: ' + entries[i].duration + '\n');
    }
  }

  function init() {
    var ptr1, ptr2;

    performance.mark('mark1');
    ptr1 = $('#testClass > .find-me');
    performance.mark('mark2');
    ptr2 = $('#testClass').find('#find-me');
    performance.mark('mark3');

    performance.measure('with selectors', 'mark1', 'mark2');
    performance.measure('selector+find ', 'mark2', 'mark3');
    showMeasurements();
    performance.clearMeasures();
  }

  $(document).ready(init);
</script>
</body>
</html>
```

The preceding code measures the speed of two different jQuery snippets. Both snippets return a jQuery object that points to the same element: the sole anchor tag with a class of find-me. There are faster ways to find the element, and we will get to these ways later, but right now, we wish to address a problem with our measuring technique.

When the code is run, it displays two measurements in the console. The first measurement is about the time it took to find the jQuery object using selectors. The second measurement is about using an id selector combined with the find() method. The second method is more optimized and should be faster.

The problem is most noticeable when you run the test code repeatedly. The timings of each run will vary, but they can vary so much that sometimes, the code that should be faster is slower. Run the timing code again, and suddenly it will become faster. What's going on? Well, although JavaScript is single threaded and we can't interrupt our code, the browser is not single threaded, nor is the operating system. Sometimes, something else on another thread can occur while our test code is running, causing it to appear to be slower. What can we do to fix this?

The answer is to use the law of averages and execute our code enough times to even out the occasional hiccups. With that in mind, here is an improved version of our timing code. The markup is the same as the previous version; only the code within the `<script>` tags has changed:

```
<script type="text/javascript">
  function showMeasurements() {
    console.log('\n');
    var entries = performance.getEntriesByType('measure');
    for (var i = 0; i < entries.length; i++) {
      console.log('Name: ' + entries[i].name +
        ' Duration: ' + entries[i].duration + '\n');
    }
  }

  function multiExecuteFunction(func) {
    var ndx, counter = 50000;
    for (ndx = 0; ndx < counter; ndx += 1) {
      func();
    }
  }

  function init() {
    performance.mark('mark1');
    multiExecuteFunction(function () {
      var ptr1 = $('#testClass > .find-me');
    });
    performance.mark('mark2');

    multiExecuteFunction(function () {
      var ptr2 = $('#testClass').find('#find-me');
    });
    performance.mark('mark3');
```

```
    performance.measure('with selectors', 'mark1', 'mark2');
    performance.measure('selector+find ', 'mark2', 'mark3');
    showMeasurements();
    performance.clearMeasures();
}

  $(document).ready(init);
</script>
```

In the new version of the code, the only thing we change is how we call our jQuery code. Instead of calling it just once, we pass it to a function that calls it thousands of times. The actual number of times the code should be called is up to you. I like to call it somewhere between 10,000 and 100,000 times.

Now we have a pretty straightforward and precise way of measuring the speed of our code. Keep in mind that we shouldn't deploy our performance-measuring code with our production website. Let's take an in-depth look at jQuery selectors so that we can understand how using the right one can make a dramatic improvement in our code's performance.

jQuery selectors

The first thing to understand about selectors is that they are a call to the browser's Document Object Model, or DOM, and that all interactions with the DOM are slow. Even developers who know the DOM is slow sometimes don't understand that jQuery uses the DOM like all of the code, which renders the markup to the browser page. Selectors are at the heart of jQuery, and small differences in selectors can make big differences in the speed of the code. It is important for us to understand how to write selectors that are fast and efficient.

Using IDs over other selectors

The fastest selectors are those that are based on the fastest underlying DOM code. A fast DOM-based element finding method is `document.getElementById()`, so it follows that the fastest jQuery selector is the one based on the `id` selector.

This doesn't mean that you should put IDs on every element in your markup. You should continue to use IDs on elements when it make sense to do so and use `id` selectors to find them or elements close to them quickly.

Caching your selectors

Every call to jQuery to evaluate a selector is a significant investment of processing time. jQuery must first parse the selector, call DOM methods to execute the selector, and finally, convert the results into jQuery objects. Remember that the DOM is slow. Luckily, you can cache your selector. Your code will still get hit with a time penalty the first time it is called, but subsequent calls are as fast as they can be.

This method works as long as you aren't performing heavy DOM manipulation. By heavy, I mean adding or removing elements from the page or other things that make the cached selector invalid.

Optimizing selectors

All selectors are not created equal. Choosing the right one can make a big difference in your application's performance, but choosing the right selector can be tricky. The following are a few tips to help you create the right selector. And remember, when in doubt about performance, measure it.

Right to left

Deep in the core of jQuery is the Sizzle selector engine. Sizzle reads from right to left. So, your most specific selector should be on the right side. Imagine that we are trying to find a `<p>` tag with a class of `bubble`. How could we optimize the selector? Let's look at an example:

```
var unoptimized = $('div.col-md-4 .bubble');
```

Our first attempt looks pretty good. But we know that we should have the most specific selector in the rightmost position, so we change things up a bit in our second example:

```
var optimized = $('.col-md-4 p.bubble');
```

In most browsers, this will be slightly faster than the first example. In previous versions of jQuery, the difference was greater. Don't worry, though; we still have more optimizations.

Reducing overly specific selectors

As developers, we tend to overdo things sometimes. This is especially bad when defining selectors. If you add more selectors than required in order to find the element you are looking for, you make jQuery do more work than required. Try to reduce your selectors to only what is required.

Let's look at an example:

```
// Too specific - don't do this
var overlySpecific = $('div.container div.row div.col-md-4
p.bubble');
```

This selector adds more specificity than is needed, making it slower than the previous example. Your selectors should be specific enough to find the desired elements, and no more.

Narrowing your search

By default, jQuery will search the entire document, looking for matches to your query. Help it out by narrowing your search.

What if we want to be faster still without polluting our markup with excessive IDs? We take advantage of the nearest parent tag that has an ID to the following:

```
var fastOptimized = $('#testClass').find('.bubble');
```

Other jQuery optimizations

The optimizations to come can be better termed rules of thumb. They will make your code faster but not drastically so. And luckily, they are easy to follow.

Updating to the latest version

Updating to the latest version is probably one of the easiest things you can do in order to speed up your jQuery code. You should always exercise care when upgrading to a new version of jQuery, but the upgrades usually bring improved speed, in addition to new features. Now that you know how to measure the performance of your code, you can measure it before and after changing versions to see whether things improve.

Don't expect huge changes in performance and read the release notes to see whether there are any breaking changes.

Using the correct version of jQuery

Currently, there are two branches of jQuery: the 1.x branch and the 2.x branch. You should only use the 1.x branch if you need to support an old version of Internet Explorer. If your website runs only on modern browsers and Internet Explorer 9 is the oldest version you need to support, you should switch to the 2.x branch of jQuery.

The 2.x branch of jQuery eliminates support for Internet Explorer 6, 7, and 8 and all of the headaches that came with it. This makes the code execute a bit faster and also makes the library smaller so that it downloads quicker.

Don't use deprecated methods

Deprecated methods are those methods that the jQuery development team has decided to remove in a future version. It can take years for the method to be actually removed. You should remove such methods from your code as quickly as possible. The reason for the method's deprecation may not be performance, but you can be sure that the jQuery team isn't going to waste time optimizing a method marked as deprecated.

Using preventDefault() when appropriate

The fastest code is the code that doesn't run. The default behavior of an event, once it is handled, is for it to be passed to the parent element and then to its parent again and again, until the root document is reached. All of this bubbling takes time and could be wasted time if you've already done all the required processing.

Luckily, it is easy to prevent this default behavior by calling `event.preventDefault()` from within your event handler. This stops unnecessary code from executing and speeds ups your app.

Never modify the DOM in a loop

Always remember that accessing the DOM is a slow process. Access it in a loop and you will compound the problem. It is better to copy the section of the DOM into JavaScript, modify it, and then copy it back. In this example, we are going to modify a DOM element and then compare it with nearly identical code that modifies an element that is not in the DOM:

```
function showMeasurements() {
  console.log('\n');
  var entries = performance.getEntriesByType('measure');
  for (var i = 0; i < entries.length; i++) {
    console.log('Name: ' + entries[i].name +
      ' Duration: ' + entries[i].duration + '\n');
  }
}
```

```
function multiExecuteFunction(func) {
  var ndx, counter = 50000;
  for (ndx = 0; ndx < counter; ndx += 1) {
    func();
  }
}

function measurePerformance() {
  console.log('\n');
  var entries = performance.getEntriesByType('measure');
  for (var i = 0; i < entries.length; i++) {
    console.log('Name: ' + entries[i].name +
      ' Duration: ' + entries[i].duration + '\n');
  }
}


function init() {

  // unoptimized, modifying the DOM in a loop

  var cnt = 0;
  performance.mark('mark1');

  var $firstName = $('.myForm').find('#firstName');
  multiExecuteFunction(function () {
    $firstName.val('Bob ' + cnt);
    cnt += 1;
  });
  performance.mark('mark2');

  // Second optimized, modifying a detached object

  var myForm = $('.myForm');
  var parent = myForm.parent();
  myForm.detach();
  cnt = 0;

  var $firstName = $('.myForm').find('#firstName');
  multiExecuteFunction(function () {
```

```
        $firstName.val('Bob ' + cnt);
        cnt += 1;
    });

    parent.append(myForm);
    performance.mark('mark3');

    performance.measure('DOM mod in loop ', 'mark1', 'mark2');
    performance.measure('Detached in loop', 'mark2', 'mark3');
    measurePerformance();
}

$(document).ready(init);
```

In the preceding code, all of the action is in the `init()` method. We are modifying the value of an `<input>` tag. In the first unoptimized pass, we modify the DOM in the loop. We do some smart things, such as caching the selector into a variable before the loop begins. This code seems pretty fast at first.

In the second pass, we detach the elements from the DOM before we begin manipulating them. We actually have to write more code in order to do this. First, we cache the form into a variable named `myForm`. Then, we cache its parent into a variable as well. Next, we detach `myForm` from the DOM using jQuery's `detach()` method.

The code in the loop is identical to that in our first version. Once we exit the loop, we append `myForm` to its parent in order to restore the DOM. While there is more JavaScript code in the second version, it is about 5 times faster than the first. This is the kind of performance boost that is always worth pursing.

jQuery isn't always the answer

jQuery is the most popular JavaScript open source library ever. It is used in more than 60% of the top 100,000 websites. But that doesn't mean that you should always use jQuery; plain JavaScript is sometimes a better choice.

Using document.getElementById

When you want to find a DOM element that has an ID, it is faster to call the `document.getElementById()` DOM method than use jQuery. Why? Because that is exactly what jQuery will do after it interprets your selector. If you don't need a jQuery object and only want the element, save yourself a few precious microseconds and make the DOM call yourself. Calling it is easy:

```
var idName = document.getElementById('idName');
```

The method accepts one parameter: the name of the `id` element. Note that it doesn't have a hashtag in front of the name. This isn't jQuery. If the element is found, a reference to an element object is returned. If it is not found, `null` is returned. Again, remember that the returned value is not a jQuery object, so it won't have jQuery methods attached to it.

There are other native browser methods available and, in general, they are faster than the code written in JavaScript whether it is jQuery, your own code, or code in some other library. Two other methods are `document.getElementsByTag()` and `document.getElementsByClassName()`. They return an `HTMLCollection` object, which is any array-like collection of elements. If no match is found, the collection is empty and has a length of zero.

> Older browsers, such as Internet Explorer 8, don't have `document.getElementsByClassName()`. So, if you need to support older browsers, you should check whether this method exists before you use it. jQuery is smart enough to use the native browser's version if it is present or its own code if it is missing.

Using CSS

jQuery and JavaScript are useful for many things, but they shouldn't be used for everything. Things such as animating, rotating, transforming, and translating DOM elements can often be done smoother and faster with CSS. jQuery has some methods that use CSS. However, by writing your own CSS, you can obtain results customized to your needs. CSS can take advantage of the host system's **graphics processor unit (GPU)** to produce results that no amount of jQuery/JavaScript can reproduce.

Summary

We started this chapter by learning how to measure our code's performance. We then put that knowledge to use by measuring the speed of different selectors as we learned how to write better and faster selectors. We also learned some jQuery best practices that improve our code's speed. We ended the chapter by realizing that jQuery isn't always the answer. Sometimes, better code comes from using plain old JavaScript or DOM methods.

In the final chapter, we will introduce jQuery plugins. Plugins are bits of amazing functionality all wrapped up in easy-to-use packages. Functions allow us to easily add graphical widgets, such as calendars, sliders, and photo carousels, to our apps. We will learn how to use plugins, where to find them, and finally, how to write our own plugin.

10
Benefiting from the Work of Others with Plugins

In the previous chapter, we learned how to time our code and then about things we can do to improve the performance of our jQuery code. With that out of the way, let's turn our attention in the tenth and final chapter about jQuery plugins. Plugins hold true to the jQuery motto of write less, do more. They enable you to take advantage of the work of others and easily plug their work into your app.

In this chapter, we will learn about jQuery plugins. In the core of jQuery is its prototype object. A plugin is an object that extends the jQuery prototype object enabling new features in all jQuery objects. jQuery has an officially supported set of UI plugins called jQuery UI. There are thousands of free plugins available but finding the good ones requires patience and caution. Here are the things we will cover in this chapter:

- Finding and installing plugins
- jQuery UI
- Writing your own plugins
- Plugin best practices

Finding plugins

If you click on the **Plugins** menu on any of jQuery's websites, you will be taken to the jQuery Plugin Register. Although the site does have a lot of plugins, they are old and haven't been updated in years. Not to worry, the folks at the jQuery Foundation decided that given their limited resources there was no point in packaging plugins themselves. The Internet already has a few popular package managers; two of the more popular ones are npm and Bower. The jQuery team recommends that plugin publishers switch to using npm.

The Node Package Manager, or npm, was originally just for providing packages for the Node.js web framework. But their ease of use and native cross-platform ability has led to npm's adoption as a package manager for all manner of applications. Many command-line tools, mobile frameworks, and other utility applications are implemented as npm modules. It is no wonder that the jQuery team made it the package manager of choice for jQuery plugins as well.

Finding jQuery plugins on npm is easy. Simply go to the website at `https://www.npmjs.com/`. In the search box, enter `jquery-plugin`. At the time of writing, there were more than 1,200 jQuery plugins available. Finding plugins is easy; it is harder to decide which of the many plugins to use.

Imagine that you are looking for a tooltip plugin. Ignore, for this example, that there is a plugin in the jQuery UI library. The first thing you would do is enter `jquery-plugin tooltip"` in the npm search bar. What kinds of questions should you ask yourself before deciding to use a plugin in your code? The first might be is the project actively maintained? Others would include does it have passing unit tests? Is the source code clean and well written? Does it have dependencies on other plugins? Is there clear documentation with sample code? What kind of licensing does it use? Does it have any open issues? If the source code is on GitHub, does it have any stars?

Only after you have done your due diligence and are satisfied that it is a quality plugin should you use it in your code. The barrier for adding a plugin to npm is pretty low, so there are a lot of bad plugins. Some were built poorly, some are old and haven't been maintained, and there may even be some malicious ones out there.

 npm manages packages, not plugins. jQuery plugins are a special kind of npm package. Throughout this chapter, I will use the word plugin but I will actually be referring to an npm package containing a jQuery plugin.

Installing plugins

You have found a plugin or two that you like, so now what? Installing a plugin via npm is also easy but first you need to make sure that you have a `package.json` file located in the root of your application. This is a JSON file that is required by npm. If you don't have a `package.json` file, npm will not install your plugin. The following is an example of a rather minimalistic `package.json` file:

```
{
  "name": "plugins",
  "version": "1.0.0",
  "description": "A demo of using and writing plugins",
  "repository": "none",
  "license": "MIT",
  "dependencies": {
    "tipso": "^1.0.6"
  }
}
```

Please note that it is a JSON file and not a JavaScript object. The first field is the name of the application. Name is a required field; without it, npm will not install a package. If you are creating a plugin and plan to upload it to npm, the name must be unique.

The second field is the version number of the application. It is also required. The value placed here is very important when you are creating your own plugins. Whether or not to upgrade a plugin is based on the value of this field stored in npm when compared to the user's local copy.

The next three fields are not required but will cause warnings to be generated if they are missing when installing a plugin. The first is the description field, which is a short statement describing the app. Then there is the repository field. If there is a valid repository, it will contain a sub-object with two fields: type and URL. The type identifies the type of source control used, with values like `git` and `svn`. Finally, there is the license field, which is the type of software license the plugin is released under. Create a `package.json` file at the root of your application.

Before you can install an npm package, you will need to install Node.js. npm is included with Node.js, so head over to `https://nodejs.org/` and download and install the version for your system. Once you have installed Node, you will want to upgrade npm. I know that seems strange, but Node and npm are on different release cycles and the version of npm included with Node is usually out of date.

To upgrade npm, enter:

```
npm install npm -g
```

On Mac and Linux systems, you may need to use a sudo command. With npm installed and upgraded, you are finally ready to install a plugin. Enter the following at the terminal or command prompt:

```
npm install <name of package> --save
```

The example package.json file showed one more field: dependencies. It is a dictionary of key-value pairs. The key is the name of a package that your app is dependent upon and the value is normally its version number. This field is created for you automatically when you install packages with --save appended to the end of the command.

Care should be taken anytime you use the sudo command. It executes the command with root privileges. If the command being executed has malicious intents, it would be able to do almost anything it wanted. Instead of using the sudo command, you can set your account as the owner of the directory where npm installs packages: /user/local. Simply execute the following command once:

```
sudo chown -R $USER /usr/local
```

This is the change owner (chown) command. It sets your account as the owner of the /usr/local directory. -R tells chown to recursively walk all of the subdirectories making your account their owner as well.

Updating a plugin

Occasionally, a package that your application depends on will be improved. In order to upgrade all of your dependencies, you run the update command without specifying a package.

```
npm update --save
```

This command will check every package in your package.json file and update all of the out of date packages. When it is finished, it will also update the package.json file with the new version numbers.

If you would prefer to be a bit more surgical in your use of the update command, you can supply the name of the package you would like to update.

```
npm update <name of package> --save
```

This command will update only the package specified in the command. If it updates the package, it will update its version number in the package.json file.

Uninstalling plugins

If you ever need to delete a plugin, use the `uninstall` command. The `uninstall` command will delete a package by removing all of its files from `node_modules` and updating the `package.json` file. Think carefully before executing this command since it can't be undone. If you use the `-save` option, it will also update the `package.json` file.

```
npm uninstall <package-name> --save
```

Adding a plugin

Now that we know how to install, update, and remove npm packages, let's add the popular `m-popup` plugin to our app. It is a plugin that creates lightweight and customizable modal popups. You can find it in npm at `https://www.npmjs.com/package/m-popup`. This is the plugin's main page, where you will find lots of information about the plugin. It usually contains the author's name, the type of license, coding samples, and installation instructions. The installation instructions are usually in the upper right-hand corner. To install `m-popup`, enter the command:

```
npm install m-popup
```

Remember to execute the command from the root directory of your app and please note there is no `-g` here. The `-g` option is only used when we are installing a package globally, but this is not the case here. When we install plugins locally, it is from the root directory of our application where the `package.json` file is located.

During installation, npm creates a directory, `node_modules`, if it was not present already. Inside of it, another directory will be created, `m-popup`. The name of the directory is always the name of the package. This is part of the reason why npm packages must have unique names.

The contents of every package is different, so you might need to explore around a bit to find the files you need; generally they will be in a directory named `dist` or possibly one named `src`. We are looking for the files we need to add to our app for the plugin to work. The instructions on the package page will normally tell us the names of the files, but not the directory that they are in. In our case, we need two files, one CSS and the JS, and both are in the `dist` directory.

```
<!DOCTYPE html>
<html>
<head lang="en">
  <meta charset="UTF-8">
```

```html
    <link href="//maxcdn.bootstrapcdn.com/bootstrap/3.3.2/css/bootstrap.
min
.css" rel="stylesheet"/>
    <script
src="//ajax.googleapis.com/ajax/
libs/jquery/2.1.1/jquery.js"></script>
    <script src="//maxcdn.bootstrapcdn.com/bootstrap
/3.3.2/js/bootstrap.min.js"></script>
    <!-- These are the includes for the popup, one for CSS the other for
JS -->
    <link rel="stylesheet" href="node_modules/m-popup/dist/mPopup.min.
css"/>
    <script src="node_modules/m-
popup/dist/mPopup.jquery.min.js"></script>
    <style>
      .mPopup {
        /* popup modal dimensions */
        width: 60%;
        height: 300px;
      }
    </style>
    <title>Chapter 10 - Adding a Plugin</title>
</head>
<body>
<div class="jumbotron">
  <div class="container">
    <h1>Chapter 10</h1>
    <p>Adding a jQuery plugin is an easy way to add more
    functionality to your site.</p>
    <p><a id="displayPopup" class="btn btn-primary btn-lg"
    href="#" role="button">Display Popup</a></p>
  </div>
</div>
<!-- this is the popup's markup -->
<div id="sample1" class="mPopup">
  <button class="mPopup-close">x</button>
  <div class="popup-header">Popup title</div>
  <div class="popup-body">
    Content goes here.
    Dismiss popup by clicking the close x in the upper right
    corner or by clicking on the greyed out background.
  </div>
</div>
```

```
<script type="text/javascript">
  function init() {
    var popup = $('#sample1').mPopup();
    var button = $('#displayPopup').on('click',function(){
      popup.mPopup('open');
    });
  }
  $(document).ready(init);
</script>
</body>
</html>
```

This code links in m-popup's CSS file and its JavaScript file, then creates a CSS class, which sets the width and height for the popup modal. It would be better to move the CSS to its own file. Next, we add some HTML to the end of our markup just before the script tag.

This is the HTML that defines the popup. The class, mPopup, also makes the markup initially hidden on the page. The plugin defines two sections, header and body, represented by the classes popup-header and popup-body.

The code to activate the plugin is pretty simple.

The code waits for the document ready event then calls the init method. In the init method, we get a reference to our popup and hook the click event of the button. When the button is clicked, we call the mPopup method with a string, open, which is the name of the popup method we are calling. To exit the modal, click the **close** button in the upper right-hand corner of the modal or anywhere on the grayed-out overlay.

There is plenty more that this plugin can do. To learn more about it, you should read the plugin's package page on npm. You may even want to study its source code.

jQuery UI

The jQuery team manages a collection of UI widgets, interactions, effects, and themes called jQuery UI. This collection is a collection of plugins. The home page for the jQuery UI is http://jqueryui.com/. Let's take a quick look at what jQuery UI is and how to use it.

jQuery UI is made up of four main components: interactions, widgets, effects, and the core. Only the core is required, so the download system allows you pick just the components you want in your own customized version.

jQuery UI Interactions

Interactions are a way to make page elements come alive and able to move in new ways. For instance, you can make a div, which is draggable and droppable. Other interactions are: resizable, selectable, and sortable. Interactions may be used either individually or in combination and help you to make your site fluid and interactive. And like most of jQuery UI, interactions are easy to use. Let's see how easy:

```html
<!DOCTYPE html>
<html>
<head lang="en">
  <meta charset="UTF-8">
  <link
  href="//maxcdn.bootstrapcdn.com/bootstrap/3.3.2
  /css/bootstrap.min.css" rel="stylesheet"/>
  <script src="//ajax.googleapis.com/ajax/libs/jquery
/2.1.1/jquery.js"></script>
  <script src="//maxcdn.bootstrapcdn.com/bootstrap
/3.3.2/js/bootstrap.min.js"></script>
  <link href="jquery-ui/jquery-ui.min.css" rel="stylesheet">
  <script src="jquery-ui/jquery-ui.min.js"></script>
  <title>Chapter 10 - jQuery UI Widget Factory</title>
  <style>
    .box {
      width: 100px;
      height: 100px;
      background-color: pink;
      margin: 5px;
    }
  </style>
</head>
<body>
<div class="jumbotron">
  <div class="container">
    <h1>Chapter 10</h1>
    <p>Interactions allow you to create an interactive and fluid
    site. Click and drag the boxes around the page.</p>
      <div class="box"><h1>1</h1></div>
      <div class="box"><h1>2</h1></div>
      <div class="box"><h1>3</h1></div>
      <div class="box"><h1>4</h1></div>
  </div>
</div>
```

```
<script type="text/javascript">
  function init() {
    $('.box').draggable();
  }
  $(document).ready(init);
</script>
</body>
</html>
```

Let's walk through this example and make sure we understand what it is doing. In order to use jQuery UI, we include its CSS and JavaScript files. Then we do an inline `<style>` to make our divs look like pink boxes.

In the body section, we lay out our page, creating four pink boxes inside of a container div. Although it is a container div, it will not contain the boxes after we drag them around. The boxes are only constrained by the browser window.

In JavaScript, we wait for the document ready event; we call the `init()` method then call `draggable` on every div with a class of `box`. When rendered in a browser, this example allows you to move the numbered boxes anywhere you like so long as it is within the browser's window.

jQuery UI widgets

Widgets are interactive and customizable UI elements. jQuery UI comes with 12 widgets. Unlike HTML elements, all of jQuery UI's widgets are themeable, meaning that they can be styled and colored to match your website's design. In alphabetical order, they are: accordion, autocomplete, button, datepicker, dialog, menu, progressbar, selectmenu, slider, spinner, tabs, and tooltip.

One of the nice things about jQuery UI widgets is that, unlike HTML elements, they are customizable and themeable. You can make all of the jQuery UI widgets match. One possible problem is that not every element has a jQuery UI equivalent. One noticeable omission is the input element. But luckily, it isn't difficult to take care of this omission yourself.

```
<!DOCTYPE html>
<html>
<head lang="en">
  <meta charset="UTF-8">
  <link href="//maxcdn.bootstrapcdn.com/bootstrap
  /3.3.2/css/bootstrap.min.css" rel="stylesheet"/>
  <script src="//ajax.googleapis.com/ajax/libs
  /jquery/2.1.1/jquery.js"></script>
```

```html
<script src="//maxcdn.bootstrapcdn.com/bootstrap
/3.3.2/js/bootstrap.min.js"></script>
<link href="jquery-ui/jquery-ui.min.css" rel="stylesheet">
<link href="jquery-ui/jquery-ui.theme.min.css" rel="stylesheet">
<script src="jquery-ui/jquery-ui.min.js"></script>
<style>
  label {
    display: block;
    margin: 30px 0 0 0;
  }

  .form-width {
    width: 200px;
  }

  /* fixes the issues with the input that the button causes */
  .styled-input {
    color: inherit;
    cursor: text;
    font: inherit;
    text-align: inherit;
  }
</style>
<title>Chapter 10 - jQuery UI Widgets</title>
</head>
<body>
<div class="jumbotron">
  <div class="container">
    <h1>Chapter 10</h1>
    <p>Widgets give your site a unified themed looked.</p>

    <fieldset>
      <label for="form-select">Salutation</label>
      <select name="form-select" id="form-select" class="form-
      width">
        <option selected="selected">Mr.</option>
        <option>Miss</option>
        <option>Mrs.</option>
        <option>Ms.</option>
        <option>Dr.</option>
      </select>
```

```
        <label for="form-input">Last Name</label>
        <input id="form-input" class="styled-input form-width"
        name="value">

        <label for="form-button">Submit Form</label>
        <button type="submit" id="form-button" class="form-
        width">Submit</button>
      </fieldset>
    </div>
  </div>
  <script type="text/javascript">
    function init() {
      $("#form-select").selectmenu();
      $("#form-button").button();
      // make the input a jQuery UI widget so that it matches our
      theme
      $("#form-input").button();
    }
    $(document).ready(init);
  </script>
  </body>
  </html>
```

The preceding code creates three elements. Two jQuery UI elements: the select and the button. And it creates an input element. There is no jQuery UI input widget, but that isn't a problem for us. We use the button's creation method on the input. This mostly works except there are a few unpleasant side effects. A button's label is centered, so this makes our input centered as well. Also, a button uses a pointer cursor style, but an input normally has a text caret cursor. We fix these and a couple of other small issues with a class, "styled-text". In the end, we have three styled inputs that all match the theme of our site.

The jQuery UI widget factory

In the next section, we will write our own jQuery plugin using only jQuery and JavaScript, but before we do that let's take a look at another way to write a plugin, using the jQuery UI widget factory. Widgets, unlike regular jQuery plugins, have a standard structure enforced on them. This is good because it makes them easier to write, but on the downside it also means that in order to use them, the user must have both jQuery and the jQuery UI core, instead of just having jQuery.

You create widgets by passing them to the widget factory. Widgets are JavaScript objects. They must have a property named _create, which must be a function. This will be the function that is called to instantiate the widget. The create function is passed a this object that has two properties on it: this.element is a jQuery object pointing to current element. It is also passed this.options, an object holding all of the current option values. In order to make this clearer, let's look at some code:

```html
<!DOCTYPE html>
<html>
<head lang="en">
  <meta charset="UTF-8">
  <link href="//maxcdn.bootstrapcdn.com/bootstrap
  /3.3.2/css/bootstrap.min.css" rel="stylesheet"/>
  <script src="//ajax.googleapis.com/ajax/libs
  /jquery/2.1.1/jquery.js"></script>
  <script src="//maxcdn.bootstrapcdn.com/bootstrap
  /3.3.2/js/bootstrap.min.js"></script>
  <link href="jquery-ui/jquery-ui.min.css" rel="stylesheet">
  <script src="jquery-ui/jquery-ui.min.js"></script>
  <title>Chapter 10 - jQuery UI Widget Factory</title>
</head>
<body>
<nav class="navbar navbar-inverse navbar-fixed-top">
  <div class="container">
    <div class="navbar-header">
      <button type="button" class="navbar-toggle collapsed" data-
      toggle="collapse" data-target="#navbar"
            aria-expanded="false" aria-controls="navbar">
        <span class="sr-only">Toggle navigation</span>
        <span class="icon-bar"></span>
        <span class="icon-bar"></span>
        <span class="icon-bar"></span>
      </button>
      <a class="navbar-brand" href="#">Measuring jQuery</a>
    </div>
    <div id="navbar" class="navbar-collapse collapse">
      <form class="navbar-form navbar-right">
        <div class="form-group">
          <input type="text" placeholder="Email" class="form-
control">
        </div>
        <div class="form-group">
          <input type="password" placeholder="Password"
          class="form-control">
```

```
        </div>
        <button type="submit" class="btn btn-success">Sign
        in</button>
      </form>
    </div>
  </div>
</nav>
<div class="jumbotron">
  <div class="container">
    <h1>Chapter 10</h1>
    <p>Writing your own jQuery UI widget is pretty easy. The extra
    benefit is that you can use your widget in all of
      your apps or give it to the community.</p>
    <p><a class="btn btn-primary btn-lg" href="#"
    role="button">Learn more "</a></p>
  </div>
</div>
<div class="container">
  <!-- Example row of columns -->
  <div class="row">
    <div class="col-md-4 bosco">
      <h2>First</h2>
      <p>I am the first div. Initially I am the on the left side
      of the page. </p>
      <p><a class="btn btn-default" href="#" role="button"
      name="alpha">View details "</a></p>
    </div>
    <div id="testClass" class="col-md-4 ">
      <h2>Second</h2>
      <p>I am the second div. I begin in-between the other two
      divs. </p>
      <p><a id='find-me' class="btn btn-default find-me" href="#"
      role="button" name="beta">View details "</a></p>
    </div>
    <div class="col-md-4">
      <h2>Third</h2>
      <p>I am the third div. Initially I am on the right side of
      the page</p>
      <p><a class="btn btn-default" href="http://www.google.com"
      role="button" name="delta">View details "</a></p>
    </div>
  </div>
</div>
```

```javascript
<script type="text/javascript">
  function init() {
    // create the yada yada widget
    $.widget("rnc.yadayada", {
      // default options
      options: {
        len: 99,
        min: 50,
        message: 'yada yada ' // the default message
      },
      // passed the this context pointing to the element
      _create: function () {
        // we only operate if the element has no children and has
        a text function
        if (!this.element.children().length && this.element.text) {
          var currentLength = this.element.text().length;
          currentLength = currentLength == 0 ? this.options.min :
          currentLength;
          var copy = this._yadaIt(this.options.message,
          currentLength);
          this.element.text(copy);
          this.options.len = copy.length;
        }
      },
      _yadaIt: function (message, count) {
        var ndx, output = "", msgLen = message.length;
        for (ndx = 0; ndx < count; ndx += 1) {
          output = output.concat(message.substr(ndx % msgLen, 1));
        }
        console.log("output = " + output);
        return output;
      },

      // Create a public method.
      len: function (newLen) {
        console.log("len method");
        // No value passed, act as a getter.
        if (newLen === undefined) {
          return this.options.len;
        }
        // Value passed, act as a setter.
        this.options.len = newLen;
      },
```

```
        // begin the name with the '_' and it is private and
        // can't be called from the outside
        _privateLen: function(){
          console.log('_privateLen method');
          return this.options.len;
        }
      });
      // convert the <a> tags to yadas
      $('a').yadayada();
      // get the length of the second yada
      var len = $('a').eq(2).yadayada('len');
      console.log('len = ' + len);
      // this code won't work
      //len = $('a').eq(2).yadayada('_privateLen');
      //console.log('private len = ' + len);
    }
    $(document).ready(init);
</script>
</body>
</html>
```

The program kicks off by waiting for the document ready event. Once it is received, it calls its `init` method. We create the widget by calling `$.widget()`, which is the widget factory. Inside the object, we must define a `_create()` method. The `create` method is called with the this context holding two values: element and options. Element is a jQuery object pointing to the current element. It is important to note that this is always a single element. Even if the original selector referenced multiple elements, the widget factory passes them to us one by one. Options contain your widget's default values, if you created it and the user didn't override them.

A widget may define other methods. Private methods must start with an underscore. Private methods are not visible from outside of the widget. Attempting to call one will generate an error. Any method lacking an underscore as the first character is public. Public methods are invoked in a rather unusual way. The name of the method is passed in a string to the widget function, like the following:

```
var len = $('a').eq(2).yadayada('len');
```

The widget in the example is a bit on the whimsical side. It replaces the text in an element with the phrase yada yada. It only does so if the element doesn't have any children and has a text function. The user can replace yada yada with a more personal message. The widget also has a public method name, len, which will return the length of message rendered.

The widget factory is probably the easiest way to get started writing plugins. Having a more rigid structure makes it more Plug and Play than regular plugins, which we will look at next.

Writing your own plugin

If you want to write a plugin that you can share with the whole world, your best bet is to create a regular jQuery plugin. It is only a bit more difficult than a jQuery UI widget, but it doesn't require jQuery UI, can easily be uploaded to npm, and shared with the world. So let's turn our `yada yada` widget into a plugin.

Prep work

Before we can really get going, we need to have a few tools sitting in the wings; the first of these is Node.js. If you didn't install it earlier, you should do so now and while you are at it, be sure to update npm. Once you have done that, you will need to log in. First, see if npm shows you as logged in:

`npm whoami`

If npm displays your username, you are OK. If not, you will need to add yourself:

`npm adduser`

You will be prompted for a username, password, and e-mail address. The e-mail address will be public. Anyone browsing the npm website will be able to see it. You should only need to do this once. Your credentials will be stored in a hidden file for future reference. With our prep work out of the way, let's make our plugin then publish it.

The plugin

The structure of a plugin is very different to that of a jQuery UI widget. First, let's see the code then we'll step through it so we can understand what it is doing.

```
;(function ($) {
  //
  $.fn.yadayada = function (options) {
    var settings = $.extend({
      min: 13,
      message: 'yada yada '
    }, options);
```

```
    return this.each(function () {
      var $element = $(this);
      if (!$element.children().length && $element.text) {
        var currentLength = $element.text().length;
        currentLength = currentLength == 0 ? settings.min :
currentLength;
        var copy = yadaIt(settings.message, currentLength);
        $element.text(copy);
      }
    });
  };

  //
  function yadaIt(message, count) {
    var ndx, output = "", msgLen = message.length;

    for (ndx = 0; ndx < count; ndx += 1) {
      output = output.concat(message.substr(ndx % msgLen, 1));
    }
    console.log("output = " + output);
    return output;
  }

}(jQuery));
```

Plugins generally begin with a semicolon. This is a safety precaution. If the plugin is used in a minified website and the file that precedes it forgets to add a terminating semicolon, the code in both files will get merged together in an unpredictable but bad way. Adding the semicolon fixes this issue if it exists, and does no harm if it doesn't.

The entire plugin is wrapped in an IIFE (pronounced "iffy"), which stands for Immediately Invoked Function Expression. An IIFE allows us to protect our code from whatever environment it is invoke. Nothing outside of the IIFE can affect it except through a predetermined interface. The interface in this case is the single variable that we pass in, which is the jQuery variable. Please note that we spell it out and don't just assume it is assigned to the dollar sign; it might not be. By passing it in, we can assign it to the dollar sign for our plugin.

We only use the jQuery variable once, to create our plugin. Traditionally, plugins only assign one function to the jQuery prototype. Nothing stops you from doing so, but it is considered bad.

Inside of the actual code of the plugin, we handle our options first. In the jQuery UI widget, the framework does the grunt work of merging user options into your options. In a plugin, we have to take care of that ourselves. Luckily, we can make jQuery do the heavy lifting by using the `$.extend()` method. Here, we create our default values then merge the values from the user on top of them. The order of the parameters is very important; items are copies right to left.

Next, we set up to return the `this` object. If we don't return `this`, the user won't be able to chain our plugin. The widget factory sent us one element at a time to operate on. Unfortunately, we aren't so lucky with a plugin: we have to iterate on our own. Again, we let jQuery do the grunt work. We use the `$.each()` method. This method sends us one element at a time. The elements are actual DOM elements so we convert them into jQuery objects since the code was written initially for them. Most of the rest of the code is pretty much the same as it was in the widget.

The `package.json` file is mandatory, as we've mentioned before. The name and version number fields are required, but you should feel out as many fields as you can. It will help your users to decide if this is the right plugin for them. Here is our `package.json` file:

```
{
    "name": "yada-yada",
    "version": "0.0.1",
    "description": "An example of writing a jquery plugin",
    "repository": "none",
    "license": "MIT",
    "author":"Troy Miles",
    "main":"jquery.yada-yada.js",
    "keywords": "jquery-plugin,ecosystem:jquery,yada-yada",
}
```

Besides the required fields we include `description`, `repository`, `license`, `author`, `main` so the user will know what the `main` file is, and `keywords` so we can be found by people looking for jQuery plugins.

Now that we have both the code and the `package.json` files, let's publish our work to npm. Keep in mind if you decide to publish this code, I've already claimed the name `yada-yada`, so you can't use it. You have to come up with a unique name of your own. Navigate to the directory holding your plugin and `package.json` files. In order to publish, simply type:

```
npm publish
```

If you've done everything right, after a few minutes npm will display your plugin's name and version number and that's it. Then go to `https://www.npmjs.com/`, enter your plugin's name into the search box, and it should show up in the results list.

Best practices

If everything goes well, your plugin may be used by lots of people all over the world, so it is really important that it is well written. Here are a few tips to help make your plugin all it can be.

Preserve chaining

Chaining is one of jQuery's best features. It allows developers to do everything they want to a set of elements in one neat package. Every jQuery developer uses it, so if you break the chain, they won't like your plugin.

Use an IIFE

It is impossible for you to know what kind of environment your plugin will be used in. Wrapping the code in an IIFE may seem unnecessary but it helps to keep your code from affecting others' code and vice versa.

Add only one function to jQuery

Your plugin may be the greatest thing since the Swiss Army knife, but you should still only use one function. Even though our little example plugin doesn't need additional functions, you should only use one. If you need more, do what other plugins and pass in the name of the function as a string and call a handler inside the plugin.

Let the user theme it

jQuery is all about customization; your plugin should be too. The example plugin allows the user to change the message via options. This concept could be extended to include styles and classes. Your plugin may be incredibly useful, but if it doesn't match the rest of the user's site, they won't use it.

Test, test, test

Before you send it out into the wild, make sure your plugin is up to the task. Test on every browser you can find, think about services like `BrowserStack`, and don't forget to ask your friends and colleagues to check it out too.

Document it

No developer will use your plugin if they don't understand it. You should document it as much as possible. Publish the code somewhere public like GitHub. Add to your `package.json` file in order to make your npm page as full as possible. Be sure to include example code with as many examples as possible of using the code.

Minify it

Be like jQuery. It provides both a minified and un-minified version. Developers like to examine what's in the un-minified version and use the minified one.

Summary

Plugins are one of the most popular jQuery features. In this chapter, we learned about the switch from plugins being kept at the jQuery Plugin Repository to the new way of storing them in npm. Then we learned how to install, update, and remove plugins from our application and even what the purpose of the `--save` option.

From npm, we moved over to jQuery UI, the official support library of UI widgets. We learned how to use them and how to create a customize download of only the widgets we want.

The last topic we tackled was how to write our own plugin. We explained each of the steps necessary to create a plugin and explained why we should let jQuery do most of the heavy lifting. We ended by showing how to upload our plugin to npm so that others can benefit from our work.

We began this book by learning why jQuery was created: to make cross-browser web development easier. In *Chapter 2, jQuery Selectors and Filters* we used jQuery's selectors and filters to find elements on the page then manipulated those elements in the following chapter. We've used events to make our site interactive and animation to make it snazzy. We learned how to get validated form data and send it to the server. We learned techniques to write clean and fast code in *Chapter 8, Writing Code that You can Read later*, and *Chapter 9, Faster jQuery*. And we finished things up by learning to use and write plugins.

jQuery is still an important part of modern web development. Although browsers have become more web-standards compliant over the years, jQuery still makes development easier. There is one area where jQuery doesn't help: writing big web apps. Frameworks like Angular or Ember or a library like React are much better choices when writing large web applications.

Index

optimizing 126
overly specific selectors, reducing 126
protocol-relative URLs 10, 11
reading, from right to left 126
search, narrowing 127
tag selectors 13
jQuery UI
about 139
interactions 140, 141
URL 139
widget factory 143, 147
widgets 141-143

L

lorem pixel
URL 55

M

minified version, jQuery
versus un-minified version 6
Model-View-Controller (MVC) 99

N

Node.js
URL 135

O

of-type selectors
:first-of-type selector 22
:last-of-type selector 23
:only-of-type selector 23

P

performance.mark() 117
performance.measure() 117
performance.now() 117
performance tests
jQuery, measuring 119-125
writing 116-119

placeholder 73, 74
plugins
adding 137, 139
finding 134
installing 135, 136
uninstalling 137
updating 136

Q

queries
chaining 23

R

ready event 42, 43

S

separation of concerns (SoC) 99-101
showMeasurements() method 119

T

tag selectors 13
Test Driven Development (TDD) 109
tooltips 72, 73

U

unit tests
about 108
using 109
writing 109-112
unwanted characters
filtering 82

V

validation 75-82

W

W3C (World Wide Web Consortium) 12

Thank you for buying
jQuery Essentials

About Packt Publishing

Packt, pronounced 'packed', published its first book, *Mastering phpMyAdmin for Effective MySQL Management*, in April 2004, and subsequently continued to specialize in publishing highly focused books on specific technologies and solutions.

Our books and publications share the experiences of your fellow IT professionals in adapting and customizing today's systems, applications, and frameworks. Our solution-based books give you the knowledge and power to customize the software and technologies you're using to get the job done. Packt books are more specific and less general than the IT books you have seen in the past. Our unique business model allows us to bring you more focused information, giving you more of what you need to know, and less of what you don't.

Packt is a modern yet unique publishing company that focuses on producing quality, cutting-edge books for communities of developers, administrators, and newbies alike. For more information, please visit our website at www.packtpub.com.

About Packt Open Source

In 2010, Packt launched two new brands, Packt Open Source and Packt Enterprise, in order to continue its focus on specialization. This book is part of the Packt Open Source brand, home to books published on software built around open source licenses, and offering information to anybody from advanced developers to budding web designers. The Open Source brand also runs Packt's Open Source Royalty Scheme, by which Packt gives a royalty to each open source project about whose software a book is sold.

Writing for Packt

We welcome all inquiries from people who are interested in authoring. Book proposals should be sent to author@packtpub.com. If your book idea is still at an early stage and you would like to discuss it first before writing a formal book proposal, then please contact us; one of our commissioning editors will get in touch with you.

We're not just looking for published authors; if you have strong technical skills but no writing experience, our experienced editors can help you develop a writing career, or simply get some additional reward for your expertise.

jQuery for Designers Beginner's Guide

Second Edition

ISBN: 978-1-78328-453-5 Paperback: 398 pages

Design interactive websites to improve user experience by using the popular JavaScript library

1. Enhance the user experience of your site by adding useful jQuery features – provide easy navigation, communicate updates and changes, and allow site visitors to interact with content.

2. Learn the modular approach to jQuery, including the addition of plug-ins to achieve advanced effects without writing much code at all.

Developing Responsive Web Applications with AJAX and jQuery

ISBN: 978-1-78328-637-9 Paperback: 248 pages

Design and develop your very own responsive web applications using Java, jQuery, and AJAX

1. A practical guide to empower you to develop responsive web applications by combining the strengths of AJAX and jQuery.

2. Learn how to build a series of web applications on top of a website quickly and efficiently.

3. By the end of this book, you will have mastered ways with which you can leverage AJAX and jQuery as per your project needs.

Please check **www.PacktPub.com** for information on our titles

jQuery 2.0 Development Cookbook

ISBN: 978-1-78328-089-6   Paperback: 410 pages

Over 80 recipes providing modern solutions to web development problems with real-world examples

1. Create solutions for common problems using best practice techniques.

2. Harness the power of jQuery to create better websites and web applications.

3. Break away from boring websites and create truly intuitive websites and web apps, including mobile apps.

Learning jQuery

Fourth Edition

ISBN: 978-1-78216-314-5   Paperback: 444 pages

Better interaction, design, and web development with simple JavaScript techniques

1. An introduction to jQuery that requires minimal programming experience.

2. Detailed solutions to specific client-side problems.

3. Revised and updated version of this popular jQuery book.

Please check **www.PacktPub.com** for information on our titles

Lightning Source UK Ltd.
Milton Keynes UK
UKOW04f1953180117

292375UK00016B/432/P

9 781785 286353